THE GOLIARD POETS

THE GOLIARD POETS

Medieval Latin Songs and Satires

WITH VERSE TRANSLATION BY GEORGE F. WHICHER

A NEW DIRECTIONS PAPERBOOK

First published by New Directions in 1949.
First ND paperback edition, 1965.

Printed in the United States of America

New Directions books are published for James Laughlin by
New Directions Publishing Corporation
333 Sixth Avenue, New York 10014

FOURTH PRINTING

To

ROBERT FROST

for converse   common cause   and brotherhood

CONTENTS

ILLUSTRATIONS

GOLIAS AND HIS TRIBE

Unregenerate poetry was not approved at the Alsatian convent of Hohenburg, though outside its walls the twelfth century world was bursting into song. The Abbess Herrad von Landsberg, who presided over the well-born sisters of the cloister from 1167 until her death in 1195, had a poor opinion of literature unsanctioned by present piety or classical precedent. When she composed for the edification of her nuns a book of useful knowledge, calling it the *Hortus Deliciarum* or Garden of Delights, she took occasion to register her official disapproval of poets on the loose. Among several hundred miniatures drawn presumably by her own hand is one which shows in a single graphic image the low place that secular writers held in relation to the total scheme of learning.

The design, patterned after a rose window, pictures Philosophia crowned and seated on a throne in the center, with Socrates and Plato as her attendants. Around her in the seven petals of the rose stand the Seven Liberal Arts with their symbols. Outside the closed circle of knowledge and below it sit four figures at writing desks, pen in hand. The rubric informs us that these are poets and intellectuals (*poetae vel magi*). At the shoulder of each, whispering in his ear, flutters a scrawny, long-necked fowl of blackest hue, obviously Satan's emissary straight from the pit putting into the writer's mind what the Devil would have him say. Thus, as Herrad saw it, wicked notions were spread abroad in the form of heresies, ungodly rhymes, and merry tales.

It was undeniable that a surge of intellectual vitality not altogether concerned with things of the spirit was sweeping through Western Europe at the very time when the Abbess of Hohenburg was portraying the diabolical inspiration of poets. Old molds were being broken and fresh forms created. New centers of learning, the universities, served to scatter seeds of intellectual culture, and with the good corn there sprang up a due proportion of tares. The disciples and successors of Abelard, a thinker a hundred years ahead of his age, were insisting that reason as well as authority had a right to be heard, presumably to the greater glory of God, though perhaps some already were beginning to suspect that reason and authority might not always accord. In response to the new spirit vernacular literatures flowered almost overnight. Troubadours, *trouvères*, and minnesingers poured out a profusion of lyrics. Other makers, not less prolific, fashioned folk-epics, *chansons de geste*, and Arthurian romances. Roland, Lancelot, Tristram and Iseult, Aucassin and Nicolete, the heroes and heroines of idealized chivalry, came to take their places beside the patriarchs of the Old Testament and the warriors of Troy.

Latin literature also shared in the renaissance, or even anticipated it. For many men and some women in the twelfth century Latin was far from being a dead language. It was a daily and familiar speech for clerics of all descriptions, for men of law and the army of notaries, secretaries, and scribes concerned with legal matters and affairs of state, and for the horde of scholars thronging to universities and cathedral schools. Moreover it was the almost inevitable vehicle of the written word. Both King Arthur and Reynard the Fox were celebrated in the language of learning before they became popular in French, German, Dutch, or English versions. Songs composed in Latin were truly international and crossed linguistic frontiers as readily as the music that went with them.

Three types of Latin lyric were available to twelfth century scholar-poets. The prestige of the Roman classics was still powerful enough to inspire imitations of Ovid or Horace, which followed the time-honored quantitative meters of antiquity and copied closely the rhetoric of these admired models. But at the same time a new living poetry in Latin was being perfected by Christian poets, who in the course of several centuries of experimentation had brought Latin verse back to the natural patterns of accentual or rhythmic meter, accompanied by sonorous and often intricate rhymes. The writing of sequences and hymns bore fruit in an immense literature of sacred song, of which the powerful *Dies Irae* attributed to Thomas of Celano is the most famous monument, though many other fine hymns like *Jerusalem the Golden* are still familiar in translation.

A third variety of Latin lyric, which came into being before the first troubadour appeared in Provence, used verse forms borrowed from church minstrelsy to express a revived paganism and the immemorial urges of the flesh. The writers of this type of lyric could not help being aware that they were using a tongue dignified by ancient usage. The characters and words formed by their pens were the same that Virgil and Cicero, St. Jerome and St. Augustine had once employed. But they drew their inspirations less from memories of classic or Christian authors than from the immediate tenderness and passion of medieval life. Their relation with sacred writ was frequently flippant. Unconsciously or by intention prepense they were protesting against the theological distrust of the body. Many, if not all, the poems of this description were produced by writers currently known as Goliards or of the tribe of Golias. It was perhaps the notoriety of this school, as recently exemplified in a disreputable rhymer who called himself the Archpoet, which prompted the Abbess Herrad to level her prim rebuke at secular authors.

The origin of the term *goliard* is far from clear. Perhaps *gula*, gluttony, was the germ from which it sprang. But it must soon have gathered to itself, snowball fashion, various other associations. Among these were implications derived from the Philistine giant

Goliath, whose name in the Latin of the Vulgate appears as Golias. We perhaps need to be reminded that Goliath was only one of a whole brood of giants issuing from Gath, sons of Harapha, with whom the Israelites struggled for forty days and forty nights. He and his monstrous kindred came to be considered types of wickedness and diabolical evil, just as David, the ancestor of Jesus, became an antecedent symbol of Christ. *Venit enim verus David Christus, qui contra spiritalem Goliath, id est, contra diabolum pugnaturus, crucem suam ipse portavit.* These interpretations, popularized by lections from the breviary, were drawn ultimately from a sermon attributed to St. Augustine, though actually by Caesarius of Arles.

It was apparently in the sense of an adversary of righteousness, a sort of Antichrist, that Bernard of Clairvaux stigmatized Abelard as a Golias and Arnold of Brescia as his armor-bearer. Possibly, as someone has suggested, the followers of Abelard may have taken to speaking of themselves as the sons of Golias in derisive allusion to Bernard's name-calling, but there is no evidence to support this supposition.

Meanwhile, since Goliath was the opponent of the shepherd boy David, his name could be aptly applied to any foe of shepherds. Probably the earliest use of the term *gens Goliae*, the tribe of Golias, is to be found in a mock-elegy on a sheep by Sedulius Scottus. What the poet had in mind was evidently just such prowling outcasts and sheep-lifters as Mak in the *Second Shepherds' Play*. It would be an easy step from this to apply the name to any sort of thief and vagabond, and eventually to fix it upon vagrants of a particular type, the *clerici vagi* or wandering scholars. Golias eventually became a kind of eponymous hero, typical of the greedy, half-starved reprobates who traveled light with threadbare cloaks and a few staves of Latin verse as their only baggage.

Hedge-priests, monks out of the cloister, men who for one reason or another had left the schools and taken to a nomadic life, had been a trouble to the church since the fifth century. These *vagantes* or *gyrovagi* were greatly increased in number when the universities came into being and began to draw crowds of students from far and near. The young scholars soon fell into a way of traveling from one school to another, as the contemporary saying went, seeking the liberal arts at Paris, law at Orleans, medicine at Salerno, magic at Toledo, and manners and morals nowhere. Many of them were attracted less by love of learning than by hope of sharing the privileges and perquisites of a scholarly life. The professions were soon overstocked, and living by the wits became common. The Goliard poet was commonly an expert beggar. Sometimes he was worse.

By the beginning of the thirteenth century vagabond scholars had become a pest which had to be sternly dealt with. The councils of the period contain frequent directions for their suppression. Goliards were commonly linked with jugglers, buffoons, and other low strollers. When they could be caught, they were to be deprived of the tonsure,

[3]

thus making them in effect outlaws with no place in the social order. Apparently these measures were successful, since the Goliards quickly lost status and at length ceased to exist altogether. By the fourteenth century they were only a name of reproach. When Chaucer called his miller "a janglere and a goliardeys," he meant that the man was a foul-mouthed babbler.

In their heyday, about 1160, the Goliards were the ecclesiastical equivalent of jongleurs and court jesters. They wrote Latin poems that were not essentially different from what the jongleurs were writing in the vernacular. In fact the same person might write at one time as a clerk and at another as an entertainer for the unlearned. In the former capacity he was prepared to supply special diversion for Latin-speaking audiences, and his highest ambition was to win a post in the official household of some prince of the church. The *Cambridge Songs*, which were written down about 1050, indicate how miscellaneous was the stock in trade of an early Goliard. The relation of the Archpoet to his patron, the Archbishop of Cologne, is representative of what every Goliard desired, though few attained it.

The body of Goliardic verse contains many diverse elements and is not marked by any such consistency of attitude as is perceptible in the lyrics of the troubadours. It includes crusading hymns, a few genuinely religious lyrics, and many restatements of classical themes. But nowhere is there any trace of courtly love. The clerk knew not the refinements of the gentle heart. His approach was more direct. On occasion the Goliards turned poetic forms developed for churchly purposes to most uncanonical use in celebrating the joys of the flesh and the pleasures of the tavern. At other times they scourged the greed and corruption of the clergy and satirized the failings of monks. Perhaps the formula that most nearly comprehends their poetry is anything and everything that might offend the pious. Speaking generally, they were rebels against authority and sometimes against decency.

What may be called the first movement of Goliardic verse was innocent and natural enough, ranging from the hearty pleasure of the Irish Sedulius (a "displaced person," not a wandering scholar) in mutton and ale to the more sophisticated delight of later clerkly poets in nature, souvenirs of the classics, and the charms of rustic maidens. Their favorite object of attack was the uncultivated layman. Their constant thesis was the superiority of the clerk to the soldier in the lists of love. It is not necessary to attribute lyrics of this type to ribalds and vagrants. Any poet with a tincture of learning might produce such pretty trifles in an idle moment. Doubtless many pieces of the sort were written by young men who later became grave churchmen. The worst that can be said of Goliardic poetry at this stage is that it contained the first intimations of that reviving independence of judgment and worldliness that were to mark the later and greater Renaissance. Of its authors Robert Frost has said that

> singing but Dione in the wood
> And *ver aspergit terram floribus*
> They slowly led old Latin verse to rhyme
> And to forget the ancient lengths of time,
> And so began the modern world for us.

But with Primas of Orleans and the Archpoet we encounter types of the learned vagabond whose disreputable living was humorously reflected in their writings. Primas, a hanger-on of the schools, was seldom out of trouble, fleeing from town to town of northern France and securing patronage as much perhaps by the menace of his bitter tongue as by the admiration due to his considerable talents. The Archpoet celebrated in the guise of his famous confession the irresistible attractions of wenching, gaming, and drink. These two poets more than any others created the conventional image of the Goliard as a libertine and a reckless wanderer, begging favors with a clever rhyme. Literary fancy seems to have added the notion of an *ordo vagorum* or hobo poets' guild as a kind of burlesque of the religious brotherhoods.

Burlesque and parody were often employed in Goliardic productions. Both sacred and profane poets delighted in puns and neat plays on words, but the Goliard became a specialist in substituting sly irreverences in hymns and offices. At times the turning of Biblical phrases to secular uses may have been almost unconscious, the result of the poet's exclusively ecclesiastical education. Thus a learned lyrist might use the words, "though I speak with the tongues of men and of angels," to introduce a poem on a kind of love which could not by any stretch of the imagination be included within the apostolic meaning of charity. More intentionally mischievous, no doubt, was the alteration of a hymn to the Virgin, beginning

> Verbum bonum et suave

into a lip-smacking song in praise of wine —

> Vinum bonum et suave.

Parody quickly degenerated into outrageous blasphemy and vileness. Certain canons in council indicate that brazen persons, Goliards or jesters or other buffoons, had to be restrained from singing profane or silly responses in church. The impulse to mock at the solemnities of liturgical ceremony gave rise to a whole series of parodies under such titles as the *Drunkards' Mass*, the *Office of the Ribalds*, the *Gluttons' Mass*, and so on, in French as well as in Latin, where *bibamus* took the place of *oramus* and the benediction was "Fraud be with you."

A second main wave of Goliardic poetry, which may have been stimulated by the moral satires of Walter of Châtillon, attacked the avarice and laxness of both the secular and regular clergy, sparing none from the Pope down. Simony was, of course, a special target for reprobation, but no sins that could possibly be laid to priests and monks were omitted. The decay of sound learning was a frequent cause of lamentation. Very little of this satirical literature rose above the commonplace, and it now inspires only antiquarian interest.

The best and most characteristic Goliardic poems are those dedicated to waywardness, either a simple sensuous delight in spring and the satisfaction of love, or an almost frenetic ecstasy in the joys of the tavern. Perhaps no finer song in praise of drinking has ever been written than the verses beginning "Meum est propositum" from the *Confession of Golias*. In commenting on the bibulous *In taberna quando sumus*, Miss Helen Waddell exclaims: "It seems not possible that poetry should be as gay as this. These poets are young, as Keats and Shelley and Swinburne never were young, with the youth of wavering branches and running water." There is indeed a kind of childlike insouciance in this and some other pieces, which has a flavor only approximated in some late Latin authors, such as Apuleius. The paganism of Horace bears the burden of pagan melancholy, the *carpe diem* note, from which most Goliardic writing is exempt. These poets have no thought for the morrow and no dread of distant drums. They are the beneficiaries of a Christian society even though they repudiate its responsibilities.

The Age of Faith included both renegades and parasites, since catholic Christianity embraced not a selection of certain human types and qualities, but all that is humanly possible. It is a cardinal mistake to think of the twelfth and thirteenth centuries exclusively in terms of the Crusades, Thomas à Becket, Chartres cathedral, St. Francis, Thomas Aquinas, and Dante. The great structure of mystical belief and scholastic logic which these climactic centuries reared would be incomplete without its arabesques of fruit and flowers and its gargoyle faces. These were supplied by the Goliards, and their work also breathes the spirit of a creative moment.

Fortunately not all conventual societies followed the lead of Herrad von Landsberg in discountenancing the graceless muse. The monks of Benedictbeuern in Bavaria gave shelter to a manuscript anthology of secular Latin verse, which contained not only the *Confession of Golias* but likewise many kindred productions by Latin-speaking writers who exercised their learning in the composition of love songs, drinking songs, parodies, satires, and other amusements. From about the year 1275 until the early nineteenth century this collection lay perdu in the library of the monastery, a cuckoo's egg in the nest of Holy Church. One would like to know how many brothers in the course of five centuries relieved the boredom of a life of austerity by turning its unsanctified pages.

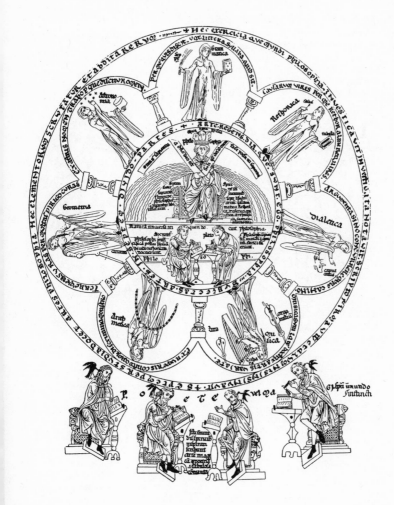

SEDULIUS SCOTTUS

SEDULIUS the Irishman, a precursor of the wandering scholars, was not a
university man in search of a living, but a learned refugee, presumably
a monk, driven from his native shores by Norse invaders. On the wings
of a great wind, as he tells us, he arrived at Liège, where Bishop
Hartgar allowed him and his two companions to inhabit a dark,
tumbledown dwelling, "a house fit for moles." Very shortly the
bishop was in receipt of a plea for repairs, couched in vigorous hendec-
asyllables. More Irish fugitives joined the band, until Sedulius found
himself at the head of a little group of *sophoi*, proud of their erudition
and their piety, whom he addressed affectionately as "four-horse team
of the Lord, and light of the people of Ireland." Between 850 and 875,
approximately, Sedulius wrote in classical meters and in reasonably
pure Latin a large number of courtly poems extolling his patrons,
eulogizing certain Carolingian princes and noblewomen whose favor it
behooved him to cultivate, and occasionally recording such events as a
notable victory over the Danes or an outbreak of the plague. Among
these formal offerings are a few lively personal lyrics, including several
requests for largess in the form of mutton or liquor. This is the aspect
of his writing which most definitely places him in line with the later
Goliardic poets. In other respects he is not typical: he did not use
rhyming accentual verse, nor did he, even mentally, sport with
Amaryllis in the shade. In 881 the Vikings sacked Liège. We have no
inkling of Sedulius' fate, but from the general holocaust some at least
of his writings emerged unscathed. A copy of St. Paul's epistles in
Greek, preserved at Berne, is thought to be written in his own hand.

Flamina Nos Boreae

Flamina nos Boreae miro canentia vultu
   perterrent subitis motibus atque minis:
tellus ipsa tremit nimio perculsa pavore,
   murmurat et pelagus duraque saxa gemunt,
aereos tractus Aquilo nunc vastat iniquus
   vocibus horrisonis murmuribusque tonans,
lactea nubifero densantur vellera caelo,
   velatur nivea marcida terra stola,
labuntur subito silvoso vertice crines
   nec stat harundineo robur et omne modo,
Titan, clarifico qui resplendebat amictu,
   abscondit radios nunc faciemque suam.
Nos tumidus Boreas vastat — miserabile visu —
   doctos grammaticos presbiterosque pios:
namque volans Aquilo non ulli parcit honori
   crudeli rostro nos laniando suo. —
Fessis ergo favens, Hartgari floride praesul,
   sophos Scottigenas suscipe corde pio:
scandere sic valeas caelestia templa beatus,
   aetheream Solimam perpetuamque Sion.

Praesulis eximii clementia mensque serena
   flamina devicit rite superba domans.
Suscepit blandus fessosque loquacibus austris
   eripuit ternos dapsilitate sophos;
et nos vestivit, triplici ditavit honore
   et fecit proprias pastor amoenus oves.

A Great Wind — Enter Sedulius

White squalls from the north, amazing to behold,
Scare us with sudden gusts and threats of cold.
Earth itself shakes, fearing to be so blown,
Old ocean mutters, and the hard rocks groan.
The unruly north wind hollows the vast air,
Its hoarse voice now whines here, now bellows there.
Stray milkwhite fleeces thicken into cloud,
The faded earth puts on a snowy shroud.
From wooded hills great boughs are shorn off short,
Oaks cannot bend like reeds, nor find support.
The sun, which lately shone with dazzling blaze,
First dims his beams, then wholly hides his face.
Fierce Boreas rifles us — distressful sight!
We pious priests and scholars erudite,
The swooping blast spares not our dignities,
Its cruel beak tears all that it can seize.
O Hartgar, flower of bishops, from its rages
Save with all zeal these wayworn Irish sages;
So may you mount to temples of the blest,
To heavenly wisdom, Zion's endless rest.

The bishop, rare soul, calm and benevolent,
Found means to tame the boisterous element.
The three philosophers, bounteously he used them,
And when they tired of talking, soon excused them;
Nor clothes nor honors has he since refused them.
Like a good shepherd, ever generous,
Sheep of his pasture he has made of us.

Nunc Viridant Segetes

Nunc viridant segetes, nunc florent germine campi,
nunc turgent vites, est nunc pulcherrimus annus,
nunc pictae volucres permulcent aethera cantu,
nunc mare, nunc tellus, nunc caeli sidera rident.

Ast nos tristificis perturbat potio sucis,
cum medus atque Ceres, cum Bachi munera desint;
heu! quam multiplicis defit substantia carnis,
quam mitis tellus generat, quam roscidus aether.

Scriptor sum (fateor), sum Musicus alter et Orpheus,
sum bos triturans, prospera quaeque volo,
sum vester miles sophiae praeditus armis:
pro nobis nostrum, Musa, rogato patrem.

Drought In Spring

Now green are the cornfields and bloom is on every bough,
The vineyards are now in bud, the best of the year is now,
The air is soft with the songs of motley birds the while;
Now sea, now land are smiling, now stars in heaven smile.

But ours is a bitter potion — the saddening truth is this:
We're out of mead and beer, and Bacchus' gifts we miss.
Alas, what manifold shrinkings the fleshpots are subject to!
And the earth so prodigal of fruits, and the air of dew.

I'm a writer (I own it), an Orpheus, a second Musicus, I.
I'm the ox that treads out corn — may someone profit thereby!
Yes, I'm your knight of learning, armed with a poet's pen.
Muse, ask our good father bishop: when do we drink again?

Tado, Benigne Vide

Tado, benigne vide vatis pia vota canentis:
    "Vive deo felix saecla futura videns."
Te docet — euge — papam domini doctrina docentem,
    sensibus in vestris sunt satis artis opes.
Angelus angelicam Rafael medicus medicinam
    conferat et vitae tempora longa tuae,
opilio domini serves ut ovile superni
    per solis cyclos, pastor ovilis ovans;
denique stelligeri conscendas culmina caeli
    praesul ab angelicis ductus ad astra choris.
Emicat ecce dies paschalibus alma triumphis,
    in qua congaudent sidera rura salum.
Salve, festa dies, festarum sancta dierum,
    qua deus infernum vicit et astra tenet.
Tellus en vario pandit sua munera partu
    spondens agricolae vincere posse famem.
Surrexit Christus sol verus vespere noctis,
    surgit et hinc domini mystica messis agri.
Nunc vaga puniceis apium plebs laeta labore
    floribus instrepitans poblite mella legit,
nunc variae volucres permulcent aethera cantu,
    temporat et pernox nunc philomela melos,
nunc chorus ecclesiae cantat per cantica Sion,
    alleluia suis centuplicatque tonis.
Tado, pater patriae, caelestis gaudia paschae,
    percipias meritis limina lucis: ave.

Easter Greetings

Tado, a poet's greetings here behold,
Pray view them kindly, every period:
May you live long, and may you see unrolled
Age after age to come, happy in God.

The poet shows you — O most excellent! —
Teaching the lessons of the Master here,
Well fitted for the task by native bent,
And blest in blessing like a father dear.

The angel Raphael, heaven's physician, poured
Angelic powers of healing on your head,
And gave you length of days to serve the Lord
As shepherd, that the sheep might still be fed.

Your zeal for souls a very sheepfold stands,
Where year by year the flock is folded fast;
And you shall mount, borne up by angels' hands,
Our patron saint above the stars at last.

See now the day of paschal triumph gleam,
Which heaven and earth and sea alike adore.
Hail, holy day, above all days supreme,
When God spurned hell and reached the stars once more.

The giving of earth's bounty has begun,
A sign of hope to husbandmen it is.
Lo, Christ has burst from darkness, our true Sun
Rises — the mystic harvest-home be His.

'Mid Tyrian flowers plebeian bees prolong,
Knee-deep in sweets, their toilsome wanderings;
Now myriad birds stipple the air with song,
And Philomel, night-long, tunes her throat and sings.

Now too in church glad hymns of Zion rise
And, hundred-voiced, the alleluias swell.
See, father of your flock, before you lies
The light of endless Easters. Fare you well.

Nos Sitis Atque Fames

Nos sitis atque fames conturbat, bestia duplex,
    vulnificis rostris nos laceratque suis.
Nec nos oblectat praedives copia rerum,
    sed nos excruciat horrida pauperies;
nec nos oblectant dulciflua dona Liei
    mellifluusque medus domata nostra fugit;
nec nos oblectat cacavis biscoctaque Mosa,
    flavicomae Cereris gratia dulcis abest.
Tenuida nos macerat, crudelis bestia, sophos;
    optime Christe, rogo, respice nos, domine:
nec gustu facilis, nulli potabilis ipsa
    est quia nec Cereris dulcida progenies;
non est Iordanis, non amnis filia Mosae,
    sed torrens Cedron turbidus hanc genuit.
Haec sophicae mentis cunctas obnubilat artes,
    laetitiam removet tristitiamque gerit;
flavicomum Cereris mentitur habere colorem:
    di, talem terris hanc removete feram;
Laetheo fluvio vosmet summergite monstrum
    seu Stigiis undis condite tale nefas,
illic quo valeat crudeles solvere poenas:
    quae nos excruciat, praemia digna luat.
Quid moror in verbis ventosque lacesso querelis?
    O pater, has geminas, obsecro, vince feras;
large salutiferum contra vulnuscula, praesul,
    Sedulio famulo da cataplasma tuo.

Ast his versicolis risit pius ille relectis
    ac sophicis votis prospera cuncta dedit.

Small Beer

Now thirst and hunger, that two-headed beast,
Vexes with ravening beaks scholar and priest.
We cannot think our stores are plenteous
While horrid shortages discomfort us;
No wine, free-flowing, tempts us to carouse,
Mead that is born of honey shuns our house,
The Meuse, twice boiled, gives no zest to the pot
Where gold-haired Ceres' choicest boon is not.
Small beer, that fell beast by the wise abhorred,
Besets us now. Good Christ! relieve us, Lord!
Unfit to taste or swallow is our brew,
A spurious brat which Ceres never knew:
No daughter, this, of Meuse or Jordan flood,
Brook Kedron sired it, hence it's full of mud;
Thus, roily, it beclouds the learned mind,
Banishes joy and leaves remorse behind.
O false-gold fraud! small beer of smallest worth!
Ye gods, remove this blemish from the earth!
The abortion, quick, in Lethe's wave submerge,
Or bid the Styx arise and work a purge.
This griping drench — the foul fiend guard it well —
May take first prize among the pains of hell.
Vain words! O father, what more can I say?
Our twin affliction you alone can slay:
Your man Sedulius, scoured by this disaster,
Asks from your generous hand a healing plaster.

The bishop read these lines, the plea succeeded,
He laughed, the saint, and gave us all we needed.

Aut Lego Vel Scribo

Aut lego vel scribo, doceo scrutorve sophian:
  obsecro celsithronum nocte dieque meum.
Vescor, poto libens, rithmizans invoco Musas,
  dormisco stertens: oro deum vigilans.
Conscia mens scelerum deflet peccamina vitae:
  parcite vos misero, Christe Maria, viro.

A Scholar's Life

I read or write, I teach or seek for lore:
  I wait on my Lord God both night and day.
I feed, I freely drink, and rhyme the more,
  When fast asleep I snore, when wakeful pray.
My soul, knowing life's corruptions, grieves therefor:
  Save, Christ, O Mary, save a hapless castaway.

THE CAMBRIDGE SONGS

HALF a hundred poems of all descriptions, the repertory of a Goliardic minstrel living somewhere near the junction of the Rhine and the Moselle, were copied on ten parchment leaves by an English traveler about the year 1050 and brought back to the monastery of St. Augustine at Canterbury. Four pieces too erotic for the taste of the monks were at some time erased with the knife or blotted out with oak-gall. Since the latter part of the seventeenth century the manuscript has been in the library of Cambridge University, and hence the poems have come to be known as the Cambridge Songs. Actually the bulk of them are of German origin, products of the literary renaissance that reached its height in the later tenth and early eleventh centuries. Two of the poems, however, are known to be by St. Fulbert of Chartres (d. 1029), and others are not improbably of French or even of Italian composition. The collection is of the most heterogeneous kind. Metrically it includes pieces in classical meters, including scraps from Virgil, Horace, and Statius; a second group are in the form of sequences imitated from the liturgical chants developed in the monastery of St. Gall; and still others are cast in popular accentual meters or rhymed stanzas, which could be written indifferently in Latin or the vernacular. In substance about one fifth of the Cambridge Songs are religious and one fifth historical or personal. Among the remainder are a number of versified folktales or humorous anecdotes, such as the story of Johan the Monk, and poems on spring and love, including the beautiful *Levis exsurgit Zephirus*. The Goliard who compiled and used this interesting collection was prepared to satisfy all tastes.

Vestiunt Silve

Vestiunt silve tenera merorem
virgulta, suis onerata pomis;
canunt de celsis sedibus palumbes
    carmina cunctis.

Hic turtur gemit, resonat hic turdus,
pangit hic priscos merula sonores;
passer nec tacet, arridens garritu
    alta sub ulmo.

Hic leta canit philomela frondis,
longas effundit sibilum per auras
sollempne; milvus tremulaque voce
    ethera pulsat.

Ad astra volat aquila; in auris
alauda canit, modulos resolvit,
de sursum vergit dissimili modo,
    dum terram tangit.

Velox impellit rugitus hirundo,
clangit coturnix, graculus fringultit;
aves sic cuncte celebrant estivum
    undique carmen.

Nulla inter aves similis est api,
que talem tipum gerit castitatis
nisi que Christum baiulavit alvo
    inviolata.

A Summer Song Of Birds

Delicate leafage decks the gloom of woodlands,
See how the boughs with fruit are heavy laden;
High in the tree-tops all the pigeons perching
    Murmur their carols.

Moaning of doves and thrushes' flutelike music
Blend with the blackbirds' never changing whistle;
Sparrows unquiet, high beneath the elm-tree,
    Laughingly chatter.

Glad in the branches nightingales are singing,
Hark! in the air the notes prolonged and stately
Vibrate; the kite is shaking down from heaven
    Tremulous outcries.

Up to the stars the eagle soars; the lark too
Rises in air and frees his tuneful measures;
Sweet is his mounting song, he sings another
    Earthward descending.

Sounding his clamor, darts the rapid swallow,
Quail like to drum, while shrill the jackdaws twitter;
Everywhere singing, all the birds together
    Honor the summer.

Think of the bee, for not a bird is like him,
None is a type of chastity more perfect,
Only excelled by her whose spotless bosom
    Pillowed the Christ-child.

In Vitis Patrum Veterum

In vitis patrum veterum
quiddam legi ridiculum,
exemplo tamen habile;
quod vobis dico rithmice.

Iohannes abba, parvulus
statura, non virtutibus,
ita maiori socio,
quicum erat in heremo:

"Volo," dicebat, "vivere
secure sicut angelus,
nec veste nec cibo frui,
qui laboretur manibus."

Respondit frater: "Moneo,
ne sis incepti properus,
frater, quod tibi postmodum
sit non cepisse satius."

At ille: "Qui non dimicat,
non cadit neque superat."
ait, et nudus heremum
inferiorem penetrat.

Septem dies gramineo
vix ibi durat pabulo;
octava fames imperat,
ut ad sodalem redeat.

Qui sero, clausa ianua,
tutus sedet in cellula,
cum minor voce debili
appellat: "Frater, aperi:

"Iohannes opis indigus
notis assistit foribus;
nec spernat tua pietas
quem redigit necessitas."

Johan The Monk

In holy fathers' lives of old
A most amusing tale is told,
Yet not without its moral too;
I'll set it down in verse for you.

Johan the monk was far from tall,
But towered in virtue over all.
Once he addressed in fervent mood
The monk who shared his solitude.

"I wish," he said, "to shape anew
My life and live as angels do,
And what the angelic life demands
Is clothes and food not made by hands."

The elder monk replied: "My brother,
Be not more hasty than another
To undertake through vain self-will
Vows that you cannot well fulfill."

But he: "A risk is not a sin;
Risk nothing, nothing lose or win."
With that he shed his monkish dress
And naked ranged the wilderness.

Seven days of eating grass for forage
So filled his mind with thoughts of porridge
That, overcome by famine's pain,
He sought his brother monk again.

The latter lay snug in his cell;
'Twas late, the door was fastened well,
When with a voice grown weak and thin
Johan called: "Brother, let me in.

"Johan your friend, grown desperate,
Stands at this well-remembered gate;
Be not so godly as to spurn
A man whose need makes him return."

Respondit ille deintus:
"Iohannes, factus angelus,
miratur celi cardines;
ultra non curat homines."

Foris Iohannes excubat
malamque noctem tolerat,
et preter voluntariam
hanc agit penitentiam.

Facto mane recipitur
satisque verbis uritur;
sed intentus ad crustula
fert patienter omnia.

Refocillatus domino
grates agit et socio;
dehinc rastellum brachiis
temptat movere languidis.

Castigatus angustia
de levitate nimia,
cum angelus non potuit,
vir bonus esse didicit.

The other answered from within:
"Johan's an angel free from sin,
At heaven's gate he stands entranced,
Nor cares how men are circumstanced."

Johan was forced to camp outside,
The livelong night he must abide;
And thus he paid one penance more
Than he had ever bargained for.

When morning dawned he was let in
With scorching words of discipline,
But all rebukes he bore with patience
His thoughts were so intent on rations.

Refreshed and warmed, he thanked the Lord
And next his mate at bed and board;
Then hoed the garden, at long last,
With arms made weaker by his fast.

Thus he was taught by sharp distress
Not to indulge in flightiness.
No angel now, the monk Johan
Tries hard to be a better man.

Iam, Dulcis Amica

Iam, dulcis amica, venito,
quam sicut cor meum diligo;
intra in cubiculum meum,
ornamentis cunctis onustum.

Ibi sunt sedilia strata,
et domus velis ornata,
floresque in domo sparguntur
herbeque fragrantes miscentur.

Est ibi mensa apposita,
universis cibis onusta;
ibi clarum vinum abundat
et quicquid te, cara, delectat.

Ibi sonant dulces symphonie,
inflantur et altius tibie;
ibi puer et docta puella
pangunt tibi carmina bella.

Hic cum plectro citharam tangit,
illa melos cum lyra pangit;
portantque ministri pateras
pigmentatis poculis plenas.

Non me iuvat tantum convivium
quantum post dulce colloquium,
nec rerum tantarum ubertas
ut dilecta familiaritas.

Iam nunc veni, soror electa
et pre cunctis mihi dilecta,
lux mee clara pupille
parsque maior anime mee.

Ego fui sola in silva
et dilexi loca secreta;
frequenter effugi tumultum
et vitavi populum multum.

Karissima, noli tardare;
studeamus nos nunc amare,
sine te non potero vivere;
iam decet amorem perficere.

Quid iuvat deferre, electa,
que sunt tamen post facienda?
Fac cita quod eris factura,
in me non est aliqua mora.

Invitation To A Mistress

Nay, come and visit me, sweet friend,
Heart of my heart, this prayer I send:
Enter, I beg, my little room
So trimly decked — you know for whom.

There stand the chairs, in each a cushion,
And lovely curtains in addition;
About the house are scattered flowers
And scented herbs most sweet in bowers.

There likewise is the table set
Where dainties brought from far are met;
There clear and plenteous wines invite you,
And all things else, dear, to delight you.

And while we dine, sweet sounds shall come
From high-pitched pipe and punctual drum;
Skillful performers, girl and boy,
Will play the songs you most enjoy.

His quill will twang the cither's wire,
Her hand will pluck the sweeter lyre,
While servants from full platters pass
Spiced wine in cups of colored glass.

No joys that banquets can afford
Can match our converse afterward,
For one choice intimacy brings
Delights that cause no surfeitings.

Sweet sister, come — my only goal
And choicer portion of my soul,
Dear beyond all, light of my eyes,
My hope, my joy, my life, my prize.

"I've been alone in darkling woods,
Seeking the deepest solitudes;
I've fled from voices time and again
And kept aloof from sight of men."

No more delay, dearest, permit;
Love is our book — let's open it.
Without you I am scarce alive,
Only by loving can we thrive.

Why not be brave and say that you
Will do soon what you're bound to do?
What sense is there in hesitating?
Come, precious — I'm not good at waiting.

Levis Exsurgit Zephirus

Levis exsurgit Zephirus
et sol procedit tepidus;
iam terra sinus aperit,
dulcore suo diffluit.

Ver purpuratum exiit,
ornatus suos induit;
aspergit terram floribus,
ligna silvarum frondibus.

Struunt lustra quadrupedes
et dulces nidos volucres;
inter ligna florentia
sua decantant gaudia.

Quod oculis dum video
et auribus dum audio,
heu, pro tantis gaudiis
tantis inflor suspiriis.

Cum mihi sola sedeo
et hec revolvens palleo,
sic forte caput sublevo,
nec audio nec video.

Tu saltim, Veris gratia,
exaudi et considera
frondes, flores et gramina;
nam mea languet anima.

A Woman Sighs In Spring

Lightly the west wind stirs in play,
The sun grows warmer day by day,
Earth bares her bosom and repeats
The melting proffer of her sweets.

The spring with purple dignified
Comes forth, wearing his robes of pride,
To scatter flowers about the land
And bid the leaves in woods expand.

Each little beast now digs his den,
The sweet birds build their nests again;
Rejoicing in the flowery wood
They shout for very lustihood.

All this I see before my eyes,
I hear, I hear their joyful cries,
And yet the happiest notes they sing
Set my lips to quivering.

When musing thus I sit alone,
Pale grow my cheeks as marble stone,
And if I raise my head, ah me!
Nothing I hear, nothing I see.

O grace of spring, at least give ear
And bless whatever quickens here:
Keep leaves and flowers and grass from blight.
For me — I weary of the light.

AUTHOR UNKNOWN,

Abelard, the most seminal thinker of the twelfth century, was likewise a poet. The verses inspired by his passion for Heloise were, as he said, spread abroad and became the talk of Paris, yet seemingly they have vanished from the earth. His surviving religious poems are metrically dexterous but rigidly correct in feeling.

It is not unlikely that some of the missing love poems may have found their way anonymously into the Benedictbeuern manuscript (later to be described), but attempts to identify as Abelard's any of the poems in that collection have as yet met with little success. Nevertheless the late Professor Philip Schuyler Allen of Chicago was rash enough to single out eight examples of learned love lyric so notably superior to the general run of love-and-springtime ditties that he believed they must be the work of an exceptional poetic genius, a genius who could be no other than Peter Abelard. This surmise is not a compelling reason for ascribing these eight poems to Heloise's lover, but it does supply a basis for grouping them together as illustrative of the highest development of the scholarly love lyric in the twelfth century.

If we are to suppose that all these poems were written by the same hand, we shall be put to it to reconcile their divergencies of attitude. They might perhaps have been composed by such a young scholar-lover as the one pictured in Hawthorne's *Rappaccini's Daughter*, whose Beatrice was an ambivalent symbol of blessedness in female form combined with a fatal but alluring poison. The poems seem to be the product of a mind tortured by intrusions of sexual desire which it can neither wholly welcome nor wholly dismiss. Now frigid, now lascivious, now blissful, now agonized and bitter, it runs through the gamut of emotions. The author (assuming that only one is in question) was a master of medieval learning and a highly trained rhetorician. The poetic structures reared by him under the painful tension of conflicting feelings are as distinctive as the love songs of John Donne.

A number of qualified judges have suspected that the *Dum Diane vitrea* and the *Hebet sidus* might be two of Abelard's lost lyrics. The latter seems to contain a clue, albeit a far-fetched one, when it declares that the name of the loved girl shines with "Phoebean light." On the high authority of Max Manitius this is to be taken as a play on words linking the Greek *helios* (the sun) with *Heloise*. May be so.

A sentence in Abelard's *Historia calamitatum suarum*, to the effect that "whatever poems he was henceforth to make should treat of love, not the secrets of philosophy," seems to have given rise, according to Professor Stephen Gaselee, to a strange notion of eighteenth century French savants that Abelard was responsible for the *Roman de la Rose*.

POSSIBLY PETER ABELARD

Such a supposition, of course, is groundless, but the absurdity would disappear if one substituted the poem *Si linguis angelicis*, which has long been recognized as one of the precursors of the great French allegory of courtly love. This Latin poem of a lover and a rose might well be by Abelard. Moreover its idealization of a frank and happy companionship between lover and beloved stamps it as an original conception of no small distinction.

The problem of the authorship of these eight love poems may never be satisfactorily solved, but it will harm no one to bear in mind while reading them the great tragic love story of the period.

Dum Diane Vitrea

Dum Diane vitrea
sero lampas oritur,
et a fratris rosea
luce dum succenditur,
dulcis aura zephyri
spirans omnes etheri
nubes tollit;
sic emollit
vi chordarum pectora,
et immutat
cor, quod nutat
ad amoris pignora.
Letum iubar hesperi
gratiorem
dat humorem
roris soporiferi
mortalium generi.

O quam felix est
antidotum soporis,
quot curarum tempestates
sedat et doloris!
Dum surrepit clausis
oculorum poris,
gaudio equiparat
dulcedini amoris.

Morpheus in mentem
trahit impellentem
ventum lenem,
segetes maturas,
murmura rivorum
per arenas puras,
circulares ambitus
molendinorum,
qui furantur somno
lumen oculorum.

Post blanda Veneris
commercia
lassatur cerebri
substantia.

Moonlight Sonata

When Diana's gleaming lamp,
Upward gliding, rises late,
Kindled while her brother's light,
Fading, still is roseate,
Sweet airs blowing from the west
Lift the mists that congregate
Far aloft:
Like music soft
Twilight soothes the breast,
And after long repelling
The heart gives love a dwelling.
Welcome then
To mortal men,
Hesperus, shining bright,
Brings cool and damp
The sleep-compelling dews of night.

O what bliss it is!
Sleep, the antidote,
From storms of care and grief
How sheltered, how remote:
Sleep that slyly enters
The portals of the eyes,
Bringing joys that equal
Sweet love's paradise.

When Morpheus has passed
To drowsy fancy sending
A light wind blowing,
Ripe corn bending,
Rippling waters flowing
Over pure sands,
Millwheels turning
While still the mill stands, —
Then robbed of all discerning
The eyes close at last.

After the subtle interchange of love
The nerves, late overtaxed,
Are now relaxed;

Hinc caligantes
mira novitate
oculi nantes
in palpebrarum rate!
Hei, quam felix transitus
amoris ad soporem,
sed suavior regressus
soporis ad amorem.

Ex alvo leta fumus
evaporat,
qui capitis tres cellulas
irrorat.
Hic infumat oculos
ad soporem pendulos,
et palpebras
sua fumositate
replet, ne visus
exspatietur late.
Unde ligant oculos
virtutes animales,
que sunt magis vise
ministeriales.

Fronde sub arboris amena,
dum querens canit philomena,
suave est quiescere,
suavius ludere
in gramine
cum virgine
speciosa.
Si variarum
odor herbarum
spiraverit,
si dederit
thorum rosa,
dulciter soporis
alimonia
post defessa Veneris
commercia
lassis captatur,
dum installatur.

A wondrous newness we are conscious of,
While eyes afloat
With darkness brimming
Glide like a boat
On eyelids skimming.
Heigh, 'tis joy to disencumber
Thought from coils of love in slumber,
But sweeter far the reawaking
Out of sleep to new love-making.

From glad satiety such fumes arise
As cloud the three-celled brain;
These vapors then incline the heavy eyes
To sleep again,
Filling the eyelids with a drowsy smoke
That holds in check the power of sight;
The animal spirits, ministering, wrap tight
The eyes as with a cloak.

Then under pleasant boughs,
While grieving Philomel descants,
Sweet it is to drowse,
Or still more sweet perchance
To woo some pretty creature on the lawn:
Spicy garden odors breathing,
Roses round our couch enwreathing,
To snatch delight in slumber's sustenance,
Love's fainting joys a while forgone
In languor deep withdrawn.

O in quantis
animus amantis
variatur vacillantis!
Ut vaga ratis per equora
dum caret anchora,
fluctuat inter spem metumque dubia,
sic Veneris militia.

But O, how many are the changes
Through which a lover's spirit ranges!
No ship that drifts
With anchor lost
Can match the shifts
Of hope and fear
Wherewith he's crossed:
The folk of Venus buy her service dear.

Olim Sudor Herculis

Olim sudor Herculis
monstra late conterens
pestes orbis auferens
claris longe titulis
emicuit;
sed tandem defloruit
fama prius celebris
cecis clausa tenebris,
Ioles illecebris
Alcide captivato.

Amor fame meritum
deflorat,
amans tempus perditum
non plorat,
sed misere
defluere
cum Venere
laborat.

Hydra damno capitum
facta locupletior
omni peste sevior
reddere sollicitum
non potuit
quem puella domuit.
Iugo cessit Veneris
vir qui maior superis
celum tulit humeris
Atlante fatigato.

Caco tristis halitus,
vel flammarum vomitus,
vel fuga Nesso duplici
non profuit;
Gerion hesperius
ianitorque stygius,
uterque forma triplici
non terruit
quem captivum tenuit
risu puella simplici.

Hercules And I

Sweat once poured from Hercules
When there were monsters to be killed
And all the land with pests was filled;
Much glory from his victories
There came to him:
But what was all his fame to him?
A flower once plucked that faded quite,
A spark soon lost in blindest night:
In Iole's arms he found delight,
A captive of her charms.

> *Love dims the worth of fame*
> *Forever.*
> *Time lost can lovers blame?*
> *O never!*
> *To sink to rest*
> *On Venus' breast*
> *They use their best*
> *Endeavor.*

The hydra, when it lost a head,
Made new ones grow, faster and faster,
That was an ugly beast to master,
Yet could not make a sign of dread
Appear in him.
Yet a mere girl put fear in him!
In Venus' power behold him lie,
The man whom gods were measured by,
Who held above his head the sky
That Atlas wearied of.

Cacus for all his filthy breath
And belching flames was done to death;
Though Nessus shaped his flight with guile,
The hero quelled him;
Geryones looked ominous,
And Hades' watchdog, Cerberus,
Three-headed both, but monsters vile
Never repelled him:
At last a simple maiden held him
A prisoner of her smile.

Iugo cessit tenero
somno qui lethifero
horti custodem divitis
implicuit,
frontis Acheloie
cornu dedit copie,
apro, leone domitis
emicuit,
truces equos imbuit
cruenti cede hospitis.

Antei libyci
luctam sustinuit,
casus sophistici
fraudes cohibuit,
cadere dum vetuit;
sed qui sic explicuit
lucte nodosos nexus,
vincitur, et vincitur
dum labitur
magna Iovis suboles
ad Ioles amplexus.

Tantis floruerat
laborum titulis,
quem blandis carcerat
puella vinculis,
quem dum lambit osculis,
nectar huic labellulis
venereum propinat;
vir solutus otiis
et gaudiis
laborum memoriam
et gloriam inclinat.

Sed Alcide fortior
aggredior
pugnam contra Venerem.
Ut superem,
hanc fugio;
in hoc enim prelio

Idle these tender bonds will keep
The man who lulled to heedless sleep
The guardian of that golden shore,
Hesperides;
Who tore from Achelous' brow
The horn of plenty, Fortune's now;
Who tamed the lion and the boar,
Great Hercules!
Even yet the savage steeds he sees
Stained with their master's gore.

Once in a wrestling match he fought
Libyan Antaeus, round on round;
He foiled the tricky foe who sought
New strength by falling to the ground,
Means to prevent those falls he found;
But he, even he who thus unwound
The toughest knot a fighter faces,
Was overcome and humbled well
When down he fell —
A mighty scion, he, of Jove —
To Iole's embraces.

Such glories clustered round his name,
Won by his deeds in many lands,
And yet a damsel overcame
And bound him fast in silken bands;
She grants the kisses he demands,
And in the play of lips and hands
He tastes the drug his passion asks;
So drunk with pleasures as with wine
He lies supine,
Oblivious of his high renown
And careless of his tasks.

Stronger than Hercules am I,
For I shall try
In arms with Venus to contend.
And to this end
I run away:
Since in this species of affray

fugiendo fortius
et levius pugnatur,
sicque Venus vincitur.
Dum fugitur, fugatur.

Dulces nodos Veneris
et carceris
blandis seris resero.
De cetero,
ad alia
dum traducor studia,
o Lichori, valeas,
et voveas quod vovi.
Ab amore spiritum
sollicitum removi.

More strength is in avoidance shown,
More lightly is the battle sped.
Thus Venus may be overthrown,
By flight discomfited.

Her dainty knots hold me no more,
Her prison door
Swings wide, the bird has flown the nest.
As for the rest,
While I'm intent
On studies somewhat different,
O my Lycoris, fare you well;
And vow this vow along with me:
To keep our love a citadel
From all disquiet free.

Axe Phebus Aureo

Axe Phebus aureo
celsiora lustrat
et nitore roseo
radios illustrat.
Venustata Cybele
facie florente
florem nato Semele
dat Phebo favente,
aurarumve suavium
gratia iuvante
sonat nemus avium
voce modulante.
Philomena querule
Terea retractat,
dum canendo merule
carmina coaptat.

Iam Dionea
leta chorea
sedulo resonat
cantibus horum.
Iamque Dione
iocis, agone
relevat, cruciat
corda suorum.

Me quoque subtrahit
illa sopori,
invigilareque
cogit amori.
Tela Cupidinis
aurea gesto,
ignem, commercia
corde molesto.

Quod mihi datur
expaveo,
quodque negatur,
hoc aveo
mente sereno.

A Morning Meditation

Now Phoebus in his golden car
    Has touched with light the hills,
The sky where his bright glories are
    With ruddy splendor fills.
From blooming flowers that deck her face
    Fair Cybele chooses one
To give in sign of Phoebus' grace
    To Semele's favored son.
To add new sweetness to the air
    The tuneful grove resounds,
The birds are vocal everywhere,
    How fresh their music sounds!
Sad Philomel for once abates
    Her tale of Terean wrong
And with her clear voice emulates
    The blackbird's merry song.

    The dance of Dione
    Echoes the gladness,
    The dancers intently
    Intoning their parts:
    Now, too, Dione,
    In frolic, in sadness,
    Lightens or crushes
    Her votaries' hearts.

    Well do I know her,
    She hinders my sleeping,
    I too am spent for love,
    Weary watch keeping;
    Sore is the heart beset
    That Cupid harrows,
    His dealings are with fire
    And golden arrows.

    What is freely supplied me
        I shudder at,
    But if aught is denied me,
        I long for that
        With constant mind.

Que mihi cedit,
hanc caveo,
que non obedit,
huic faveo,
sumque revera
felix, seu peream,
seu relever per eam.

Que cupit
hanc fugio,
que fugit,
hanc cupio;
plus renuo debitum,
plus feror in vetitum,
plus licet illibitum,
plus libet illicitum.

O metuenda
Dione decreta,
o fugienda
venena secreta,
fraude verenda,
doloque repleta,
docte furoris
in estu punire
quos dat amoris
amara subire,
plena livoris
urentis et ire.
Hinc mihi fletus abundat,
hinc fletus inundat.
Est mihi pallor in ore,
est, quia fallor amore.

Let woman grant her favor
    And I despise her,
If without hope I crave her,
    O how I prize her!
    True bliss I find
Whether she prove my comforter
Or I must die for lack of her.

She who's effusive
    I flee;
The girl who's elusive
    Suits me.
No use contending with the currents,
I'm swept away past all deterrents;
In short, the more I'm duty-ridden
The more I yearn for things forbidden.

O much to be feared
    Is Venus' reign,
Much to be shunned
    That secret bane,
Dreadful her guile
    And her chicane;
With cunning fury
    She deals the stroke,
Making men suffer
    Love's irksome yoke;
Her wrath and her envy
    Mount like smoke.
My fears abound — through her,
I'm drowned in tears — through her:
How pale is my face, how pale!
Thus it is when love's hopes fail.

Clausus Chronos

Clausus Chronos et serato
carcere ver exit,
risu Iovis reserato
faciem detexit,
purpurato
floret prato,
ver tenet primatum
ex algenti
renitenti
speciei renatum.

Vernant veris ad amena
thyma, rose, lilia,
his alludit filomena,
melos et lascivia.

Satyrus hoc excitatur
et Dryadum chorea,
redivivis incitatur
hoc ignibus Napea.

O Cupido, concitus
hoc amor innovatur,
hoc ego sollicitus,
hoc mihi mens turbatur.

Ignem alo tacitum,
amo, nec ad placitum,
utquid contra libitum
cupio prohibitum,
votis Venus meritum
rite facit irritum,
trudit in interitum
quem rebar emeritum.

Si quis amans per amare
amari posset mereri
posset amor mihi velle mederi,
quod facile sibi, tandem beare,
perdo querelas absque levare.

Time's In Prison

Time's in prison, and spring goes out,
Breaking bars that once were stout;
Open skies, softly beguiling,
Wreathe the face of earth with smiling;
In the empurpled meadow spring
Brings to bloom each growing thing,
And stands confessed, the seasons' king:
Out of winter cold and pining
Reborn with beauty shining.

Roses, lilies, every herb
Spring delights in, are renewed;
Blithely the nightingales disturb
With wanton songs the solitude.

Spring awakes the satyr's blood,
And dancing go the dryad's feet;
All the nymphs from grove and flood
Revive with spring's reviving heat.

O Cupid, love in spring is stirred
And burns with flame redoubled,
The call of spring I too have heard
And feel my spirit troubled.

I feed a hidden fire,
I love, and nought will suit,
Since my perverse desire
Longs for forbidden fruit;
Venus has set at nought
My vows to end it soon,
And has to ruin brought
One I'd have thought immune.

If just by loving till it hurts
One could be loved for his deserts,
Sure love might medicine my grief:
Easy for him, that benediction. . . .
I waste my plaints without relief.

Hoc amor predicat,
hec macilenta
hoc sibi vendicat
absque perempta.

Dum mala sentio
summa malorum,
pectora saucia
plena furorum,
semina pellere
nitor illorum.

Est Venus artibus
usa nefandis,
dum bene palliat
aspera blandis
unguibus attrahit,
omnia pandit.

Parce dato pia
Cypris agone,
et quia vincimur,
arma repone,
et quibus est Venus,
est et Dione.

For love himself declares
The stringency's intended,
'Tis right, he claims, in these affairs
And may not be amended.

When it is worst I feel
The sum of mortal ills,
Wounds that no leech can heal —
Such rage my bosom fills
That I must tax my wit
To ban the thought of it.

The wiles of Venus
Grow slyer and slyer,
She cloaks her fierceness,
Her hand creeps nigher —
Before we know it
The fat's in the fire.

Good Cyprian, hold your hand,
No more can we withstand,
We yield, and ask no other
Than peace to be between us;
We know you queen of beauty, Venus,
Be to us now love's mother.

Si linguis angelicis
loquar et humanis,
non valeret exprimi
palma nec inanis,
per quam recte preferor
cunctis Christianis,
tamen invidentibus
emulis prophanis.

Pange lingua igitur
causas et causatum;
nomen tamen domine
serva palliatum,
ut non sit in populo
illud divulgatum,
quod secretum gentibus
extat et celatum.

In virgultu florido
stabam et ameno
vertens hec in pectore
quid facturus ero;
dubito, quod semina
in arena sero;
mundi florem diligens
ecce iam despero.

Si despero merito,
nullus admiretur,
nam per quandam vetulam
rosa prohibetur,
ut non amet aliquem,
atque non ametur,
quam Pluto subripere
flagito dignetur.

Cumque meo animo
verterem predicta,
optans, anum raperet
fulminis sagitta,

Rose Of The World

Tongues of angels and of men
   Skilled in oratory
Will not serve me to express
   The surpassing glory
Whereby I am set above
   Men of every station,
Though the envious hold it leads
   Nowise to salvation.

Therefore let my tongue proclaim
   Facts and circumstances,
Yet preserve my lady's name
   Safe from all mischances;
Trust not to the public ear
   What is better hidden,
Let it to the world appear
   Secret and forbidden.

Long by that sweet flowering bush
   I stood hesitating,
What I was about to do
   Inwardly debating:
Doubtful whether seeds in sand
   I should sow, or whether
Seeking the world's flower might prove
   Desperate altogether.

Well I might despair indeed,
   There is no denying,
Since an old crone kept the rose
   Sacred from all prying,
Neither loving nor beloved,
   Thanks to this duenna —
Such a flower as Pluto snatched
   Midst the fields of Enna.

How I hoped the hag would leave
   If I bade her pray go,
Or that sudden lightning would
   Smite the old virago.

ecce retrospiciens,
vetula post relicta,
audias quid viderim,
dum moraret icta.

Vidi florem floridum,
vidi florum florem,
vidi rosam Madii,
cunctis pulchriorem,
vidi stellam splendidam
cunctis clariorem,
per quam ego degeram
semper in amorem.

Cum vidissem itaque
quod semper optavi,
tunc ineffabiliter
mecum exultavi,
surgensque velociter
ad hanc properavi,
hisque retro poplite
flexo salutavi:

"Ave formosissima,
gemma pretiosa,
ave decus virginum,
virgo gloriosa,
ave mundi luminar,
ave mundi rosa,
Blanziflor et Helena,
Venus generosa."

Tunc repondit inquiens
stella matutina:
"Ille qui terrestria
regit et divina,
dans in herba violas
et rosas in spina,
tibi salus, gloria
sit et medicina."

Let me, looking back, forget
     That old woman's strictures,
But describe the sight which yet
     Recollection pictures.

There I saw the flower in bloom,
     Queen of flowers many,
There I saw the Rose of May,
     Lovelier than any,
There I saw the brightest star
     Shine in heaven resplendent,
For whose sake I always keep
     Love for my attendant.

When I thus had seen the sight
     Long anticipated,
My unspeakable delight
     Left me much elated;
Rising up, I hastened then
     To prevent our severance,
And upon my bended knees
     Greeted her with reverence:

"Hail, most beautiful of girls,
     Gem of worth unmeasured,
Quintessence of maidenhood
     In one vessel treasured,
Hail, O dayspring of the world,
     Hail, rose of creation:
Blanchefleur, Helen of Troy,
     Venus' emanation."

In reply the star of dawn
     Spoke with accents gracious:
"He who rules the world of men
     And the heavens most spacious,
Giving violets to the grass,
     Mingling thorns and roses,
Grant you health, fame, cure of ills,
     As His will disposes."

Cui dixi: "Dulcissima,
cor mihi fatetur,
quod meus fert animus,
ut per te salvetur,
nam ego quondam didici,
sicut perhibetur,
quod ille qui percutit
melius medetur."

"Mea sic ledentia
iam fuisse tela,
dicis; nego; sed tamen
posita querela,
vulnus atque vulneris
causas nunc revela,
vis, te sanem postmodum
gracili medela."

"Vulnera cur detegam,
que sunt manifesta?
estas quinta periit,
properat en sexta,
quod te in tripudio
quadam die festa
vidi; cunctis speculum
eras et fenestra.

"Cum vidissem itaque,
cepi tunc mirari,
dicens: 'Ecce mulier
digna venerari,
hec exscendit virgines
cunctas absque pari,
hec est clara facie,
hec est vultus clari.'

"Visus tuus splendidus
erat et amenus,
tanquam aer lucidus,
nitens et serenus;
unde dixi sepius:
'Deus, deus meus,
estne illa Helena,
vel est dea Venus?'"

"Sweetest one," I said to her,
  "All my hopes assure me,
And my heart confirms my hopes,
  You're the one to cure me.
Long ago I've found this rule
  True in every letter:
He who strikes the iron hot
  Always fares the better."

"Yet you blame my fatal arms,
  Scathe and outrage feigning;
I see none, but grant there were
  Cause for your complaining,
Tell me how you got your wounds,
  All your pains revealing,
That I may, though small my means,
  Labor for your healing."

"Why should I uncover wounds
  Plain to all men's knowing?
Lo, five summers have gone by
  And the sixth is going
Since I saw one tread the dance
  Like perfection's mirror,
Like a casement when the dawn
  Clearer grows and clearer.

"I, when I had seen this sight,
  Marveled much upon her,
Saying: 'This is even she
  Worthy of all honor;
She surpasses womankind,
  Peerless among creatures,
Beauty gazing on her face
  Sees his very features.'

"Thus you came, a vision bright,
  Glory round you gleaming,
Like a sunny shaft of light
  Through the darkness streaming;
Often have I wiped my eyes,
  Saying: 'God Almighty!
Surely this is Helen, or
  Heavenly Aphrodite!'"

Aurea mirifice
coma dependebat,
tanquam massa nivea
gula candescebat,
pectus erat gracile,
cunctis innuebat,
quod super aromata
cuncta redolebat.

In iocunda facie
stelle radiabant,
eboris materiam
dentes vendicabant,
plus quam dicem speciem
membra geminabant:
quidni si hec omnium
mentem alligabant?

"Forma tua fulgida
tunc me catenavit,
mihi mentem, animum
et cor inmutavit,
tibi loqui spiritus
illico speravit;
posse spem veruntamen
nunquam roboravit.

"Ergo meus animus
recte vulneratur
ecce mihi graviter
fortuna novercatur,
nec quis umquam aliquo
tantum molestatur,
quam qui sperat aliquid
et spe defraudatur.

"Telum semper pectore
clausum portitavi,
millies et millies
inde suspiravi,
dicens: 'Rerum conditor,
quid in te peccavi?
omnium amantium
pondera portavi.'

From her fillet wondrously
  Flowed her golden tresses,
Like a snowdrift shone her throat
  Made for love's caresses,
Slender breasts like buds yet closed
  Breathed a hint ecstatic
How beyond all spiceries
  They were aromatic.

Twin stars in her happy face
  Beamed with all their brightness,
While her teeth excelled the best
  Ivory stuff in whiteness;
More than I could ever tell
  Beauty ruled her motion:
Who but she might bind the world
  In a pure devotion?

"By your radiant beauty then
  I was wholly captured,
Mind and soul and heart in me
  Felt the change, enraptured;
Though my spirit longed for speech
  With no other woman,
Strength to realize my hope
  I could never summon.

"Straightway to my very soul
  I was wounded badly,
Evil fortune from that hour
  Punished me full sadly:
Nor can anyone be more
  Grievously defeated
Than the man who, having hoped,
  Of his hope is cheated.

"Ever since I've borne the wound,
  Laboring to conceal it,
Many, many thousand times
  Have I sighed to feel it,
Saying: 'God who made this world,
  How have I offended?
Every lover's pang I've known,
  Still my woe's not ended.'

"Fugit a me bibere,
cibus et dormire,
medicinam nequeo
malis invenire.
Christe, non me desinas
taliter perire,
sed dignare misero
digne subvenire.

"Has et plures numero
pertuli iacturas,
nec ullum solatium
minuit meas curas,
ni quod sepe sepius
per noctes obscuras
per imaginarias
tecum sum figuras.

"Rosa, videns igitur,
quam sim vulneratus,
quot et quantas tulerim
per te cruciatus,
tu, si placet, itaque
fac, ut sim sanatus,
per te sim incolumis
et vivificatus.

"Quod quidem si feceris,
in te gloriabor,
tanquam cedrus Libani
florens exaltabor.
Sed si, quod non vereor,
in te defraudabor,
patiar naufragium
et periclitabor."

Inquit Rosa fulgida:
"Multa subportasti,
nec ignota penitus
mihi revelasti,
sed que per te tulerim
nunquam sompniasti;
plura sunt que sustuli
quam que recitasti.

"Food and drink I scarcely touch,
    Nor can sleep allure me,
Not a cordial can I find
    Of my ills to cure me.
Christ, desert me not, lest I
    End my sad existence,
Deign to succor in his need
    One who asks assistance.

"Long and long I have endured
    These unhappinesses,
Nor has any comfort yet
    Lessened my distresses;
Not though I have often used
    Midnight necromancy,
Picturing myself with you
    In the realms of fancy.

"Seeing how I'm wounded, Rose,
    Knowing that I suffer
Torments which on your account
    Day by day grow rougher,
Will you not, of courtesy,
    Work my restoration?
Let my trouble find in you
    Joyful termination?

"Do this, and my praise of you
    Never shall be halted,
While like cedared Lebanon
    I shall be exalted.
If in you (which God forbid!)
    I should be mistaken,
Let me perish in the wreck,
    Never more to waken."

Softly spoke the radiant Rose:
    "Many things you've told me,
Things I too have felt, if you
    Truly would behold me:
All my tenderness for you
    In your tale was slighted,
Yet my woes are more than those
    You have here recited.

"Sed omitto penitus
recitationem,
volens talem sumere
satisfactionem,
que prestabit gaudium
et sanationem,
et medelam conferet
melle dulciorem.

"Dicas ergo, iuvenis,
quod in mente geris,
an argentum postulas,
per quod tu diteris,
pretiosos lapides,
an quod tu ameris;
nam si esse poterit,
dabo quicquid queris."

"Non est id quod postulo
lapis nec argentum,
immo prebens omnibus
maius nutrimentum,
dans inpossibilibus
facilem eventum,
et quod mestis gaudium
donat luculentum."

"Quicquid velis, talia
nequeo prescire,
tuis tamen precibus
opto consentire;
ergo quicquid habeo,
sedulus inquire,
sumens id quod appetis
potes invenire."

Quid plus? Collo virginis
brachia iactavi,
mille dedi basia,
mille reportavi,
atque sepe sepius
dicens affirmavi:
"Certe, certe illud est
id quod anhelavi."

"But the numbering of my woes
    I forbear, unheeding;
Better comfort would I taste,
    Every joy exceeding,
More than healing I desire
    Satisfactions sunny
Which in sweetness I conceive
    Pleasanter than honey.

"Therefore speak your mind, young sir,
    Tell me what you covet:
Is it precious stones you wish?
    Money — do you love it?
Name the prize that you desire
    So that I may know it,
And if it be possible
    Straightway I'll bestow it."

"Neither gold nor gems I ask,
    Never could I crave them;
For the general good of all
    It were fit you gave them.
What I ask is that you grant
    Things beyond obtaining,
That my sorrowing heart may feel
    Bliss that knows no waning."

"What you wish I cannot well
    Find it out by guessing,
Though if I could grant your prayers,
    You might have your blessing:
Make account of all I have,
    Sift and search minutely,
When you find what you desire,
    Take it absolutely."

Would you more? I threw my arm
    Round her neck, down bending,
Myriad kisses gave I then
    With her kisses blending;
Then I cried, and many a time
    Have confirmed it, saying:
"Surely, surely this is it
    For which I was praying."

Quis ignorat amodo
cuncta que secuntur?
Dolor et suspiria
procul repelluntur,
paradisi gaudia
nobis inducuntur,
cuncteque delicie
simul apponuntur.

Hic amplexus gaudium
est centuplicatum,
hic meum et domine
pullulat optatum,
hic amantum bravium
est a me portatum,
hic est meum igitur
nomen exaltatum.

Quisquis amat itaque
mei recordetur,
nec diffidat illico
licet non ametur;
illi nempne aliqua
dies ostendetur,
qua penarum gloriam
post adipiscetur.

Ex amaris equidem
amara generantur,
non sine laboribus
maxima parantur,
dulce mel qui appetunt
sepe stimulantur,
sperent ergo melius
qui plus amarantur.

Who knows not the dainty things
   Unto lovers given?
Grief and sighing, pain and care
   Far away are driven;
Even the joys of Paradise
   Are by love augmented —
All delights of soul and sense
   At one time presented.

Now increased a hundredfold
   Bliss fills our embraces,
Now my lady's hopes and mine
   Share the selfsame bases.
Now for all the pains of love
   I am well rewarded,
Now moreover to my name
   Glory is accorded.

May whoever loves like me
   Think of us united,
Nor suppose that anywhere
   Love goes unrequited;
Some day surely he shall know,
   Though he scarce believe it,
His exceeding great reward,
   Yea, he shall achieve it.

Though from bitterness of soul
   Bitter fruit's engendered,
No one gains the highest prize
   Till the price is rendered;
They who long for honeycomb
   Must not flinch from bee-stings,
Let them, when their smart is worst,
   Dream of future feastings.

Sevit Aure Spiritus

Sevit aure spiritus,
et arborum come fluunt penitus,
in frigore silet cantus nemorum;
dum torpescit ver a solo,
tepet amor pecorum.
Nunquam amans sequi volo
vices temporum
bestiali more.

En gaudia felicia,
quam dulcia stipendia
sunt hec hore
nostre Flore!

Non de longo conqueror obsequio;
remuneror stipendio,
letor leto premio.
Dum salutat me loquaci
Flora supercilio,
mente satis iam capaci
gaudia concipio,
glorior labore.

Mihi sors obsequitur non aspera,
dum secreto in camera
favet Venus prospera.
Nudam fovet Floram lectus,
caro candet tenera,
virginale lucet pectus,
parum surgunt ubera
modico tumore.

A tenello tenera
pectusculo
distenduntur latera
pro modulo,
caro carens scrupulo
levem tactum non offendit,
gracili sub cingulo
umbilicum preextendit
paululum ventriculo
tumescentiore.

Something In The Wind

Now raves the spirit of the air,
The boughs of trees are blown like streaming hair,
The woodland singers all are dumb for cold,
While tardy spring creeps torpid from the mould;
Love barely moves the barnyard now.
But as a lover I had rather
Be independent of the weather
Than take my cue from bull and cow.

> *O rare excess of happiness,*
> *O sweetness born of my success:*
> *These hours, the sign*
> *My Flora's mine.*

I make no plaint that she was hard to woo;
Already I have gained my wages due,
The rich reward that fully satisfies.
Now when my Flora gives me greeting
With speaking eyebrows over sparkling eyes,
My thoughts leap forward to a lover's meeting
And all the joys thereof:
I glory in our love.

It was a lucky fate that prompted me
When to her maiden chamber I was led;
Judge how auspicious Venus chanced to be,
For there lay Flora in her naked bed.
Her dainty skin gleamed ivory white,
Her bosom shone with light excelling,
Twin aureoles seemed to hover bright
Just where the buds were swelling.

Her most delicious virgin breast
By tender flanks was bounded;
So sound she slept, not fearing harm,
Her body felt without alarm
The light caress I gave her,
So I proceeded, under favor,
To scan below that slender waist
The navel like a dimple placed,
The belly gently rounded.

O, si forte Iupiter hanc videat,
timeo, ne pariter incaleat,
et ad fraudes redeat,
sive Danaes pluens antrum
imbre dulci mulceat,
vel Europes intret taurum,
vel et hec congaudeat
rursus in olore.

O had Jove seen what I have seen,
He too would feel his ardor keen
And try his old disguises on:
As when he rained in Danae's bower,
Pouring himself in that sweet shower;
Or when he played the bullish part
To get Europa in his power;
Or this one might rejoice his heart
If he resumed the swan.

Rumor Letalis

Rumor letalis
crebro me vulnerat,
meisque malis
dolores aggregat;
me male multat
vox tui criminis,
que iam resultat
in mundi terminis.

Invida fama
tibi novercatur;
cautius ama
ne comperiatur.

Quod agis, age tenebris;
procul a fame palpebris
letatur amor latebris
et dulcibus illecebris
cum murmure iocoso.

Nulla notavit
te turpis fabula
dum nos ligavit
amoris copula;
sed frigescente
nostra cupidine,
sordes repente
funebri crimine.

Fama letata
novis hymeneis,
irrevocata
ruit in plateis.

Patet lupanar omnium
pudoris in palatium,
nam virginale lilium
marcet a tactu vilium
commercio probroso.

A Lost Lady

Pestilent rumor
Frequently maddens me,
Adding a few more
Griefs to what saddens me:
Talk of your failings
Leaves me much mortified —
Scandal's retailings
Blown about, far and wide.

Slander completely
Smears you with disclosures;
Love more discreetly,
Shun these exposures.

What you do, let darkness hide it,
Nor to public view confide it,
Love delights in secret places,
Where whispers, sweet embraces,
And all joys betide it.

Nothing was spoken
Shameful or scandalous
While an unbroken
Fondness united us.
Love's an enigma,
Cold, cold, and ashen now —
Nought but the stigma
Left of our passion now.

New love's vagaries
Gossip gladly utters;
No one contraries
Blab of the gutters.

Now to baseness prostituted
Love's fair palace is polluted;
Even so a spotless lily
Must wither, willy-nilly,
By vile hands uprooted.

Nunc plango florem
etatis tenere,
nitidiorem
Veneris sidere —
tunc columbinam
mentis dulcedinem,
nunc serpentinam
amaritudinem.

Verbo rogantes
removes hostili;
munera dantes
foves in cubili.

Illos abire precipis
a quibus nihil accipis;
cecos claudosque recipis,
viros illustres decipis
cum melle venenoso.

Mourn then the flower —
Plucked, faded, festering;
Bright but an hour
Like a star westering.
Once, O delightful!
Dove-like her girlishness —
Now turned to spiteful
Venom and churlishness.

When you are pled with,
Hot resentment fires you.
Go — go to bed with
Anyone that hires you!

Suitors loth to buy your favor
You dismiss without a quaver;
Blind men, cripples bring more money!
And you with poisoned honey,
You are man's enslaver!

Hebet Sidus

Hebet sidus leti visus
cordis nubilo,
tepet oris mei risus
carens iubilo;
iure mereo,
occultatur nam propinqua,
cordis virga florens, in qua
totus hereo.

In amoris hec chorea
cunctis prenitet,
cuius nomen a Phebea
luce renitet,
et pro speculo
servit polo: illam colo,
eam volo nutu solo
in hoc seculo.

Tempus queror tam diurne
solitudinis,
qui furabar vi nocturne
aptitudinis
oris basia,
a quo stillat cinnamomum
et rimatur cordis domum
dulcis cassia.

Tabet, illa tamen caret
spes solatii,
iuvenilis flos exaret;
tanti spatii
intercisio
annulletur, ut secura
adiunctivis prestet iura
hec divisio.

Heloise

Mounting clouds of heart's affliction
Dim my happy star;
Laughter on my lips were fiction,
Such my sorrows are:
She, the flowering spray
Gladdening my heart, the nearest
Friend of all I count my dearest,
She is stolen away.

She when maidens dance love's dances
Puts the rest to shame;
Phoebus' glorious light enhances
Her celestial name;
Heavenly lights her eyes
Ever mirror: her I cherish,
Not to cherish were to perish,
Nothing else I prize.

Now I seek with eyelids swollen
Hours for lonely grief,
I who, thanks to night, have stolen
Kisses like a thief:
Dear lips, now long gone,
How the spice of your caresses
Once perfumed my heart's recesses,
Sweet as cinnamon.

Time wears on, and hope receding
Yields no comfort yet.
Youth to age is ever speeding,
Ageless is regret.
Our division seems
Sure to last till sad disunion
Blights our love, and love's communion
Fades like fading dreams.

Notices of an extraordinary poet called Primas or the Primate keep cropping out from the middle of the twelfth century to the time of Boccaccio. The Englishman Serlo of Wilton, who may have encountered him at Paris, wrote a poem to his memory. Thomas of Capua, speaking of the three varieties of composition, instanced Cassiodorus as a model for prose, Virgil for metric poetry, and Primas for rhythmic. In Henri of Andeli's poem on the *Battle of the Seven Arts* the rear guard of Grammar's forces is marshaled by Ovid and Primas together. Salimbene the chronicler mentioned him as "a most amusing rogue and a great versifier and extemporizer," who might have lived a most useful life if he had but turned his heart to God.

The most circumstantial account comes from a certain Richard of Poitiers, a monk of Cluny, who wrote as follows under the year 1142:

In these days there flourished at Paris a certain teacher named Hugo, by his colleagues nicknamed Primas, a man of mean appearance and twisted face. From an early age he devoted himself to secular writings, and because of his wit and his knowledge of letters the renown of his name shone forth over many lands. Among all the teachers of rhetoric he was preeminent for his eloquence and for his quickness in rhyming, so much so that they say everyone was moved to hearty laughter who heard these verses, which he composed rantingly on a shabby mantle given him by a certain bishop.

The poem mentioned, the second of the four here selected for translation, is a good example of the talent for diatribe possessed by this clever, bitter, and disreputable rhymer.

Though Primas could on occasion write a respectable show-piece on such classical themes as Orpheus and Eurydice or the return of Ulysses, he greatly preferred to season his erudition with depravity. Like Swift he spared neither himself nor his readers if nastiness was in question. When the Flora of his fancy abandoned his bed, he found consolation in elaborating the thought that she was only a strumpet, and with painstaking obscenity he depicted her or such another *bona roba* aping the manners of a fine lady. He had no reluctance to portray himself as a guzzler and a gamester, the victim of his own weaknesses, a picker-up of crumbs from rich men's tables, a hateful pest whom it was a charity to kick downstairs.

But Primas cannot be lightly dismissed. He was a great craftsman in verse, a worthy forerunner of that more famous gutter poet, François Villon. An equal master of leonine hexameters, rhymed elegiacs, sequences, and tirade-rhymes — this last his specialty — he was capable of striking out new methods, of learning how to surpass himself with each successive work. Notice that the simple realistic narrative of how he was bilked by a rascally innkeeper is replaced in his later account of how he was thrown out of an almshouse for taking the part of a crippled inmate against the authorities by the most elaborate kind of dramatic realism, so that the story is now told exactly as it might be by an agitated old man in repeated bursts of recollection which overlap each other, each bringing to light new aspects of the situation. Rough comedy forms the core of the poem, but the comic framework as in Chaucer's *fabliaux* is much less important than the realistic delineation of character that envelops it.

The image of a shabby, fleeting figure spouting Latin invective was the contribution of Primas to the composite portrait of Golias.

Hospes Erat

Hospes erat michi se plerumque professus amicum,
    voce michi prebens plurima, re modicum.
Quis fuerat, taceo, si quis de nomine querat;
    sed qualis possum dicere: rufus erat.
Hic dum me recipi summa bonitate putarem,
    intravi plenum fraude doloque larem.
Me domini fratrem consanguineumve putares;
    sic domus et dominus excipiunt hilares.
Tunc dominus cepit vicibus me plangere crebris,
    illaqueare volens talibus illecebris:
"Dedecus est, Primas, quod sit quadrupes tibi solus."
    Non erat hoc pietas; fraus erat atque dolus.
Dum moror, evenit michi quadam forte dierum
    sumere plus solito forte recensque merum.
Unde piger cene post horam splendidioris
    ebrius obtabam membra locare thoris.
Hospes at astutus obliquo lumine ridet
    nutantemque parum scire videre videt.
"Non," ait, "est sanum dormire, sumus quia pleni.
    Ludere tres solidos, hospes amici, veni!"
Denariis inhians paucis misereque crumene,
    quin etiam decios, si placet, ante tene!
Ad mea dampna citus properans post gaudia cene
    proieci decios: non cecidere bene.
Hospes eos iecit michi fallaces, sibi fidos:
    infelix Primas perdidit v. solidos.
Vina dabant verne sapientes atque periti
    et "Bibe," dicebant, "ne moriari siti."
Me potasse prius de nil constante putavi:
    nunc scio, quod dampno vina fueri gravi.
Paulatim caput incipiens dimittere pronum,
    paulatim cepit perdere bursa sonum.

The Affair Of The Red-Headed Innkeeper

A host there was who oftentimes had sworn himself my friend,
Though all his loud professions came to little in the end;
And you may ask his name, but who he was I'll not declare,
Save this much I may venture: he had Judas-colored hair.
While I supposed he'd treat me well as any man alive,
I found his house a den of thieves, no better than a dive.
I might have been his brother, though no kinship I could boast,
The way they ran to welcome me, the servants and mine host,
And the latter rang the changes on a score of old laments,
Hoping with honeyed words to shake me down, to all intents:
"A single fatted calf for you! Nay, Primas, eat your fill."
You think that this was kindly said? You're wrong, he meant
   it ill.
Now on a day it happened, while I lingered in this haunt,
I tasted wine, and it was new and stronger than was wont;
Replete at length, for dinner was more gorgeous than my drench,
I only thought to lay my drunken limbs along a bench;
Then mine host, he gave a covert glance and smiled a wily smile,
He saw that I was nodding, lost to reason for a while.
"No snoozing after meals," quoth he, "a most unwholesome
   vice.
Come, honored friend, let sleep alone — risk three sous on the
   dice!"
(Desirous in his filthy pouch a few more coins to squeeze),
"Now set a main before me, even ten times if you please."
Too quickly after dinner I was tempted, to my cost;
Ten times I threw, and every time the dice fell wrong — I lost.
Mine host then threw, and luck, so coy to me, became his slave;
Poor Primas dropped a five-spot just to watch those cubes
   behave.
Then waitresses dashed up with wine, knowing and well-
   rehearsed:
"Fill up," they cried, "and wet your throat. No need to die of
   thirst."
I had believed my drinking-bout would cost me nought at all,
But reckoning in my losses made the outlay far from small.
As more and more my heavy head swayed downward toward the
   ground,
So less and less my dwindling purse gave out a prosperous sound:

Queque prius grandi residebat turgida culo,
   evacuata iacens ore tacet patulo.
Que fuit in cena fecunda loquax bene plena,
   nec vox nec sonitus mansit ei penitus.
Infelix Decius talem confundat amicum,
   qui sic nostra tulit, quod nichil est reliquum.

The purse that, ample-bottomed, sat so plump and firm before,
Now emptied and with gaping mouth lay silent on the floor;
Gone was her power to summon up a too abundant dinner,
No cheerful voice nor chink of coin could now be heard within
    her.
Bad luck at dice confound the friend, who after such professions
Thus cleaned me out, till not a sou was left of my possessions.

Pontificum Spuma

Pontificum spuma, fex cleri, sordida struma,
qui dedit in bruma michi mantellum sine pluma!

— Hoc indumentum tibi quis dedit? an fuit emptum?
estne tuum?

— Nostrum; sed qui dedit, abstulit ostrum.

— Quis dedit hoc munus?

— Presul michi prebuit unus.

— Qui dedit hoc munus, dedit hoc in munere funus.
Quid valet in bruma clamis absque pilo, sine pluma?
Cernis adesse nives: moriere gelu neque vives.

— Pauper mantelle, macer absque pilo, sine pelle,
si potes, expelle boream rabiemque procelle!
Sis michi pro scuto, ne frigore pungar acuto!
Per te posse puto ventis obsistere tuto.

On The Gift Of A Cloak

Primas

Scum of churchmen! clergy's dregs!
Pain i' the neck, who gave me
An unlined cloak to save me
From winter's cold, i' fegs!

Bystander

Who was it then presented
This — shall we say — integument?
It wasn't bought or rented?
It's yours?

Primas

      Yes, mine; I meant
Merely to say I mind it
That he who gave it tore away what lined it.

Bystander

But who then was the donor?

Primas

A certain prelate gave it me — the owner.

Bystander

He gave this gift so proud!
He might as well have given you a shroud.
For service in all weathers
What good's a cloak with neither fur nor feathers?
You'll see, when snow is driving,
You'll catch your death of cold — there's no surviving.

Primas

Poor mantle, what abuse could thin you?
No fur, no padding in you!
Think you, thus sadly aging,
To fend me from the blast, the storm's mad raging,
To shield me and protect me
So piercing cold will not affect me,
That in your keeping surely
I may withstand the wintry winds securely?

Tunc ita mantellus: — Michi nec pilus est neque vellus.
Sum levis absque pilo, tenui sine tegmine filo.
Te mordax aquilo per me feriet quasi pilo.
Si notus iratus patulos perflabit hiatus,
stringet utrumque latus per mille foramina flatus.

— Frigus adesse vides?

— Video, quia frigore strides:
sed michi nulla fides, nisi pelliculas clamidi des.
Scis, quid ages, Primas? eme pelles, obstrue rimas!
Tunc bene depellam, iuncta michi pelle procellam.
Conpatior certe, moveor pietate super te
et facerem iussum, sed Iacob non Esau sum.

The Mantle thus responded:

No pelt, no fleece is left, my fur's absconded;
Worn smooth am I, and like a head bare
My texture's threadbare.
The biting north to chill you
Will drive his lances through me fit to kill you.
There's no escaping
The wind's assault while all these holes are gaping;
A thousand vents in each direction
Will strip you of protection.

Primas

You think we're in for freezing?

The Mantle

I do, and you with cold are wheezing.
But till some fur is added,
It's little help you'll get from me, unpadded.
Know what, Primas? I together
With peltries could repel this pelting weather;
Buy furs, and thus augmented
I'll fight the storm and keep you well contented.
Your plight I pity truly,
And if I could, would help you duly,
But when it comes to hair my make-up
Is less like Esau than like Jacob.

Vir Pietatis Inops

Vir pietatis inops, cordis plus cortice duri,
dignus cum Iuda flammis Stigialibus uri!
Scariothis finem det ei deus aut Palinuri!
Pene furens tremulum fregit caput obice muri.
Cuius vero caput? Senis et propere morituri.
Si lupus est agnum, si vim faciat leo muri,
quod decus aut precium lupus aut leo sunt habituri?
Dum metuens mortem me sepius offero iuri,
auferor et rapido furor mea guttura furi.

   Verba quidem sunt severa
   et videntur esse vera,
   sed nec casta nec sincera:
   non Alecto seu Megera
    hanc habent nequiciam.
   Multos fallit sacramentis
   et seducit blandimentis:
   nec in falsis iuramentis
   nec in verbis blandientis
    habeas fiduciam.

   Requirebam meum censum
   et hoc facit hunc infensum;
   sed, dum vado per descensum,
   si teneret apprehensum,
   vir insanus extra sensum
    iugulasset propere.
   Nec pro deo nec pro sanctis
   est misertus deprecantis;
   sed ad vocem tribulantis
   dedit deus alas plantis;
    et sic cessit prospere.

   Sic res erat definita
   et mors mihi stabilita:
   si teneret me levita,
   brevis esset mea vita
    nec possum evadere.
   Si non esset levis talus,
   brevis esset mea salus.
   Sed dum instat hostis malus,
   retardavit eum palus
    et est visus cadere.

On The Danger Of Asking For One's Own

Merciless man, whose heart has an impenetrable shell,
Worthy to burn with Judas in the hottest fires of hell!
Judas' or Palinurus' end, God send to him as well!
He nearly broke a trembling head against the wall in rage.
Whose head, you ask? An old, old man's, and soon to die of age.
If wolf eat lamb, if lion in his might with mouse engage,
Would wolf or lion then deserve medals for being brave?
In fear of death I gave myself to the just gods to save,
And so got off and kept my throat from an outrageous knave.

Some words late spoken are severe
And seem to make the truth appear,
Though neither candid nor sincere.
The infamous libels that we hear
    Would scandalize a Fury!
Many, I know, his oaths deceive,
Many he coaxes to believe —
While lovers of the truth must grieve
To see what falsehood can achieve;
    But you be judge and jury.

I merely asked to have my own:
And in such frenzy he was thrown,
That if downstairs I had not flown
But let him catch me there alone,
His rage had so insensate grown
    I soon would have been strangled.
Nor would he heed my clamorings
For all the saints and holy things,
But God heard my petitionings
And lent my feet a pair of wings;
    Thus was the snare untangled.

How fatal would the event have been,
How slight the chance to save my skin,
Had that vile Levite penned me in!
My life had not been worth a pin
    If I had proved a laggard.
If of light heels I could not boast
I must have given up the ghost,
But when my foe pursued me most
He barged into the newel-post
    And visibly was staggered.

[85]

Si non esset talus velox,
Primas esset velut Pelops.
Sed, qui sedet super celos,
cui cantant dulce melos
   beatorum anime:
non concessit ius insano,
homicido, Daciano,
quod noceret veterano;
alioquin (vera cano)
   perissem celerrime.

Si non essent plantis ale,
satis esset michi male;
monstrum enim Stigiale
me vorasset absque sale.
Computabam gradus scale,
   sed non recto numero:
unus, septem, quinque, decem,
et in vanum fundens precem.
O quam pene vidi Lethem!
Nam tirannus minans necem
   inminebat humero.

Dum demitto me per scalas,
sepe clamans "Alas! Alas!"
dedit deus plantis alas;
sic evasi manus malas
   cursu debilissimus.
Quam nefandum opus egit!
Contra murum me impegit,
pene caput meum fregit.
Nunc extorrem me collegit,
cibat pane, veste tegit
   clerus nobilissimus.

Proclamabam "Heus! heus!
miserere mei deus!"
dum instaret hostis meus.
Eram enim ut Zacheus,
ipse velut Briareus
aut Herodes Galileus
   sive Dionisius.

Were it not that nimble heels suffice,
Primas would lie where Pelops lies;
But He who reigns above the skies,
To whom sweet canticles arise
　　From blessed souls in glory,
Would not allow that furious man,
That murderer, that barbarian,
To hurt a harmless veteran;
Or else (don't think me partisan)
　　You'd hear another story.

Were it not for wings upon my feet
Hard would have been my fate to meet;
The monster, breathing Stygian heat,
Would have seized me without salt to eat.
The stairs I counted, all complete,
　　But not as men intended:
One, seven, five, ten, I took in stride,
While uttering a small prayer inside,
Yet for all that I nearly died!
The bully, clamoring for my hide,
　　Close on my heels descended.

As headlong down the stairs I sped,
"Alas! alas!" I cried in dread;
God gave me wings, as I have said,
Thus from his evil hands I fled
　　In flight almost hysteric.
To push me was a dastard's act,
Since plump into the wall I smacked.
Wow! but my head was nearly cracked!
But now I'm free and still intact:
I'm housed and fed and clothed, in fact,
　　By a most noble cleric.

"Alack! alack!" how I did bawl,
"God save my soul! God save us all!"
My foe loomed near, tyrannical,
For like Zaccheus I was small,
And he was like Briareus, tall,
A very Herod to appal,
　　In stature Dionysian.

Vix evasi triste fatum.
Nunc suscepit exulatum
regni tenens principatum
et regina civitatum
 nobilis Parisius.

Multi monstrum ignorantes
vix hoc credunt admirantes
et sic dicunt indignantes,
 "Quis est iste dominus?
In qua fidit potestate,
qui de nostro bono vate,
de magistro, de Primate,
 tale fecit facinus?"

Cum recordor tristis hore,
qua volabam pre timore
et non erat locus more,
friget plenum cor horrore
nec iam credo quemquam fore,
 cui possim credere.
Adhuc ita tremo totus.
Non est locus tam remotus
ne amicus quisquam notus,
tam fidelis, tam devotus,
 in quo possim fidere.

A fearful fate I barely missed!
Now Paris offers to assist
Me fleeing from my antagonist:
The queenliest city on my list!
   I'll make a good Parisian.

Those who have seen no brute so dire
May disbelieve my tale entire,
"Who is he then?" they will inquire,
   "Tell us that we may know it:
This lord so quick to domineer,
How did he get the power here
To put our Primas in such fear,
   Our master, the good poet?"

Just to recall that awful day
When terror-struck I ran away
And there was no room for delay,
My heart still freezes in dismay;
Never again will I display
   Sweet faith in human nature.
I'm shaking yet and cannot mend;
My head, what refuge can defend?
Whoever seeks to be my friend,
Either to borrow or to lend,
He'll not persuade me in the end
   To trust his candidature.

Dives Eram Et Dilectus

Primas

Dives eram et dilectus
inter pares preelectus;
modo curvat me senectus
et etate sum confectus.
Unde vilis et neglectus
a deiectis sum deiectus,
quibus rauce sonat pectus,
mensa gravis, pauper lectus,
quis nec amor nec affectus
sed horrendus est aspectus.

Homo mendax atque vanus
infidelis et profanus
me deiecit capellanus,
veteranum veteranus,
et iniecit in me manus
dignus dici Dacianus.

Prius quidem me dilexit
fraudulenter et illexit.
Postquam meas res transvexit,
fraudem suam tunc detexit.
Primas sibi non prospexit
neque dolos intellexit,
donec domo pulsus exit.

Satis erat bonus ante
bursa mea sonum dante
et dicebat michi sancte:
"Frater, multum diligam te."

Hoc deceptus blandimento
et emunctus sum argento,
cum dolore, cum tormento
sum deiectus in momento,
rori datus atque vento.

Vento datus atque rori
vite prima turpiori
redonandus et errori:

Primas Lodges A Complaint

Primas

Once I was rich and well content,
Beloved by friends and eminent;
Now with old age my back is bent,
My span of life is nearly spent.
And so behold me, poor and shent,
Cast out by even the indigent
Who cough until their sides are rent,
Sleep hard, and get small nourishment:
Nor love nor care to them is lent,
Their future's bleak in any event.

A lying fellow, vain as vain,
Utterly faithless and profane,
A hulking chaplain threw me out;
One old man was another's bane:
He dared lay hands on me, the lout,
His hangman's hands, the hands of Cain.

How artfully the creature must
Have schemed to fill my eyes with dust!
Then when he had my all in trust
He sprung his trap, to my disgust.
Never did Primas feel mistrust
Nor dream of treatment so unjust
Till shoved outdoors by one foul thrust.

How he would flatter, cog, and sue
While I had coins to jingle too,
And he would say, the oily Jew:
"Brother, I simply dote on you."

Thus deceived like flies with honey,
And diddled out of all my money,
What a shock and grief of mind
All at once myself to find
Outcast in the rain and wind!

Now by wind and weather beaten,
I resume a life most filthy,
Up and down the country ganging;

pena dignus graviori
et ut Judas dignus mori,
qui me tradens traditori
dignitatem vestri chori
tam honesti tam decori
permutabam viliori.

Traditori dum me trado,
qui de nocte non est spado,
me de vite libro rado
et, dum sponte ruens cado,
est dolendum, quod evado.

Inconsulte nimis egi,
in hoc malum me inpegi,
ipse michi collum fregi,
qui vos linquens preelegi
ut servirem egro gregi,
vili malens veste tegi,
quam servire summo regi,
ubi lustra tot peregi.

Aberravi: sed pro deo
indulgete michi reo!
incessanter enim fleo,
pro peccato gemens meo.

Fleo gemens pro peccatis,
iuste tamen et non gratis;
et non possum flere satis,
vestre memor honestatis
et fraterne karitatis.
O quam dura sors Primatis,
quam adversis feror fatis!
Segregatus a beatis,
sociatus segregatis,
vestris tantum fidens datis,
pondus fero paupertatis.

Bitter the remorse I've eaten,
Bitter past all power to sweeten,
I'm a Judas, fit for hanging,
Since in yielding to the stealthy
Machinations of that traitor
I became a dissipater
Of your fame for hospitality
Nobly earned in this locality —
Made it lesser, nowise greater.

Trusting in that double-faced
Hypocrite (by night unchaste),
I to ruin rushed in haste;
From the Book of Life erased,
Grievously was I disgraced.

True it is the acts were heedless
That have led to my disasters;
I myself have been to blame,
Since my leaving you was needless —
Voluntarily there I came
And accepted coarse employment
Caring for the halt and lame;
Thus I left you, noble masters,
Where so long I'd found enjoyment.

I have erred: I ask of heaven
That from sin I may be shriven;
See, with sobs my breast is riven
And I groan to be forgiven.

Justly do I weep and groan
When I think of my malignity;
How indeed can I atone
For a crime against your dignity,
An affront to your benignity?
O but Primas' fate is bitter,
Fortune is a heavy hitter!
From my friends I'm separated
And with wretched outcasts mated;
Nothing but your contribution
Helps me bear my destitution.

Paupertatis fero pondus:
meus ager, meus fundus,
domus mea totus mundus,
quem pererro vagabundus.
Quondam felix et fecundus
et facetus et facundus,
movens iocos et iocundus,
quondam primus nunc secundus
victum quero verecundus.

Verecundus victum quero,
sum mendicus. Ubi vero
victum queram nisi clero,
enutritus in Piero,
eruditus sub Homero?
Sed dum mane victum quero
et reverti cogor sero,
iam in brevi (nam despero)
onerosus vobis ero.

Onerosus et quo ibo?
Ad laicos non transibo.
Parum edo, parum bibo,
venter meus sine gibbo
et contentus pauco cibo
plenus erit parvo libo
et, si fame deperibo,
culpam vobis hanc ascribo.

Vultis modo causam scire,
causam litis, causam ire,
que coegit nos exire?
Brevi possum expedire,
si non tedet vos audire.

Responsio sociorum
Nos optamus hoc audire
plus quam sonum dulcis lyre.

What a weight of want I carry!
Now for fields and funds and home
I've the wide world where I roam
Like a gipsy to and fro.
Once I was blest, long, long ago,
With wit acute, with language bold,
Joking, full of the Old Harry —
From my primacy, behold,
I am sunken and subdued:
Now with shame I seek my food.

Yes, I seek my food with shame.
I'm a beggar. And indeed
Who but kindly clerks will feed
One by all the Muses nursed,
Solidly in Homer versed?
But tomorrow when I wander
Off to seek for bread out yonder
And am forced all day to squander
And come stumbling homeward late,
You will not, I fear, grow fonder
Of me, banging at your gate.
On my head will fall the blame.

Blame me then, for I must bear it.
Will mere laymen, do you think,
Give me alms for Jesus' sake?
I can claim this modest merit:
Little do I eat or drink,
For my stomach, sadly shrunken,
When a single draught I've drunken,
Hardly holds the tiniest cake.
Whose the fault, then pray examine,
If your guest should die of famine?

Would you like to know the reason
For the quarrel and the treason
That expelled us, out of season?
I can state it briefly for you,
If to hear it will not bore you.

The Chapter replies
We prefer your most satiric
Speeches to the sweetest lyric.

Primas

Quidam frater claudo pede
est eadem pulsus ede
violenter atque fede,
ut captivus et pars prede
alligatus loris rede
a Willelmo Palamede
vel per noctem Ganimede.

Frater membris dissolutus,
qui deberet esse tutus,
(nam pes erat preacutus)
nichil male prelocutus,
sed mandata non secutus
calciatus et indutus
est in luto provolutus.

Provolutus est in luto
frater pede preacuto.
Quem clamantem dum adiuto
et putabam satis tuto,
fui comes provoluto
et pollutus cum polluto.

Provoluto comes fui
et in luto pulsus rui.
Dum pro bono penas lui,
nullus meus, omnes sui.

Adiuvabant omnes eum,
Chananei Chananeum,
Ferezei Ferezeum,
et me nemo preter deum
dum adiuto fratrem meum
nil merentem neque reum.

Solus ego motus flevi,
fletu genas adinplevi
ob magistri scelus sevi
et dolorem iam grandevi.

Primas

A certain brother lame of foot
Was banished from that very dwelling;
A brutal act was his expelling,
For like a captive, held as loot,
And bound behind the victor's chariot,
So was he seized by that Iscariot,
William, nicknamed Palamede,
At night the chaplain's Ganymede.

This brother with the crippled leg,
Whom no one else would think to bully
Since, so deformed, he could but beg,
Without a word of provocation,
Merely some rule misunderstood,
Roused William's sudden indignation;
So fully shod and dressed as fully,
Was plunged instanter in the mud.

Instanter in the mud he wallowed,
This brother with the foot deformed,
And when he cried for help, I stormed
And raged, fearing no retribution;
Sudden the selfsame outrage followed
And I was plunged in like pollution.

Thus my downfall was decreed —
Rolled in puddles like a swine!
Thus I paid for my good deed,
Paid on his account, not mine.

All men cringed at William's nod:
Canaanites with their kind agree,
Pharisees with the Pharisee.
Nobody took my side but God,
When to my brother's help I came
Who was not one least bit to blame.

No one but I would sympathize;
I wept to hear his groans and cries
That men in power could be so vicious —
And made things worse by being officious.

Quis haberet lumen siccum,
cernens opus tam iniquum?
sacerdotem inpudicum,
corruptorem meretricum,
matronarum et altricum,
servientem in mendicum,
claudum senem et antiquum,
dum distractus per posticum
appellaret replens vicum
adiutorem et amicum.

Nec adiutor est repertus,
nec sacerdos est misertus:
ita solus est desertus,
totus luto coopertus
nec, quo pedem ferret, certus.

Accusabam turpem actum
propter fratrem sic confractum,
claudum senem et contractum:
et dum dico "Malefactum,"
accusatus dedi saltum.

Accusatus saltum dedi.
Post hec intus non resedi
neque bibi nec comedi
capellani iussu fedi,
qui, quod sacre datur edi,
aut inpertit Palamedi
aut largitur Ganimedi
aut fraterno dat heredi,
aut asportant cytharedi
ut adquirat bonus credi.

Modo, fratres, iudicate
neque vestro pro Primate
aberrantes declinate
a sincera veritate:
an sit dignus dignitate
vel privandus potestate

But who could gaze on their obliquity
And keep from tears at such iniquity?
For, lo, an overbearing priest,
A whoremaster, a very beast,
Seducing village dames, at least,
While charged to minister to the needy,
Against an old man, lame and seedy,
Who, dragged seat foremost through the mud,
Bellowed to stun the neighborhood
For some kind friend to do him good.

For help and friends he had to wait.
The priest was not compassionate;
Thus he was left alone, perplexed,
Plastered with mud and desolate,
Not knowing where to hobble next.

Then I proclaimed the whole proceeding
A shocking piece of sheer ill-breeding:
An old man, lame, and nearly dying —
"For shame, for shame," I still was crying,
When out the door I too went flying.

I too went flying out the door. . . .
I have no lodgings any more,
Nothing to drink, nothing to eat;
The chaplain did it, I repeat,
Who steals as fast as he is able
Provender from the paupers' diet
To give to William Palamede,
Or gratify some Ganymede,
Or so-called nephews in their need,
Or singing girls — to keep them quiet,
So folks will think him charitable.

Now, brothers, judge: nor swayed by ruth,
Since you loved Primas in his youth,
Depart at all from strictest truth:
Should such a man be kept in office,
Or should he not be made to doff his
Much abused symbols of authority
By vote of an aroused majority?

senex carens castitate
et sacerdos honestate,
caritate, pietate,
plenus omni feditate,
qui, exclusa caritate
nos in tanta vilitate,
quorum fama patet late,
sic tractavit. Iudicate!

A dodderer, known for his lubricity,
From all precepts of priesthood swerving,
Unloved, unpitied, undeserving,
Whose utter lack of kindliness
(A failing seldom found in pastors)
Has plunged us all in this distress
And caused the unfavorable publicity
That you have heard. Judge, then, my masters!

A PHANTOM, hollow looking, meanly dressed, and racked by a consumptive cough, haunted the court of Rainald of Dassel, the archchancellor of Frederick Barbarossa and archbishop of Cologne, when that prince of the church was campaigning in Italy about the years 1161 to 1165. Announcing himself, perhaps in shameless parody of Rainald's titles, as the Archpoet and a man of tramontane birth, he proffered his services as a master of the art of letter writing (*dictamen*) and astutely begged for warm clothes and a place at table. This nameless ecclesiastical jester, outwardly resembling the Clerk of Oxford but harboring inwardly the lusts of a Falstaff, was the greatest of all the vagabond poets, granting that he was indeed the author of the *Confession of Golias*, the masterpiece of the school.

Most of what is known of him is contained in these autobiographical stanzas from another poem:

The poet of all poets the poorest paid — that's me!
Without a stitch to call my own, except what you can see,
A thing which often grieves me, while you laugh at poverty;
It's not my fault — don't think I'm poor because I want to be!

A scholar dig to earn his keep! I neither will nor can.
I come of military stock, my sire's a fighting man;
But toils of war alarmed me, so it seemed a better plan
To stay at home with Virgil when you, Paris, led the van.

To beg for bread is a disgrace, I will not ask relief,
And thieves, though much falls to their clutch, are seldom free from grief.
What is there left for me to do, who hold no lands in fief?
I won't become a beggar, and I'd hate to be a thief.

Often the pinch of poverty makes me acquisitive,
The plaints I send to learned men sound far too purposive;
But laymen cannot understand that poets have to live,
And even to me, it's plain to see, they've no rewards to give.

Among the ten poems which are all that can be attributed to the Archpoet are a number of triumphs exploiting the humor of barefaced impudence. One is a rhymed sermon supposed to be delivered before an assembly of ecclesiastical dignitaries which opens in a vein of lofty religious eloquence. But when the poet has occasion to quote Christ's words, "Give to everyone that asketh," he yields to the impulse to make an immediate application on his own behalf and the poem breaks down with a ludicrous appeal for means to enjoy the world. He could write fulsome praises of his patron, but when asked to compose an epic on the emperor's victories and get it done in a week, he objects that he cannot write to order and anyhow he is now thirsty and verses will flow only when wine inspires them. Nevertheless he did in some sort celebrate the fall of Milan. In disgrace because of some public scandal over a wench, he succeeded in rhyming himself back into favor once more, but the last poem of all shows him ill and destitute at Salerno, his clothes pawned and his cough worse than ever.

Much of the ingenuity of the Archpoet's verses is lost in translation. It is impossible to render the delicate surprise of shifted accent that gives point to leonine hexameters, as may easily be seen by comparing the original Latin of the first poem quoted with the stumbling effort to transpose the same effects literally into English. The *Confession of Golias*, moreover, is filled with mischievous parodies of Scripture, as when the poet makes the angel choir in echoing the words, "God be merciful to me a sinner," substitute *potatori* (drunkard) for *peccatori* (sinner). Such fine touches are the despair of the translator. But the larger intention of the poem may be preserved. The mock confession, dilating unctuously on the joys of the flesh while pretending to renounce them, may be recognized as one of the first signs of a reviving paganism, the faun-face leering from behind the mask of pious austerity.

Omnia Tempus Habent

Omnia tempus habent, et ego breve postulo tempus,
ut possim paucos presens tibi reddere versus.
Electo sacro presens in tegmine macro
virgineo more non hec loquor absque rubore.
Vive, vir inmense, tibi concredit regimen se,
consilio cuius regitur validaque manu ius.
Pontificum flos es et maximus inter eos es,
incolumis vivas, plus Nestore consilii vas.
Vir pie, vir iuste, precor, ut moneam precibus te,
vir racione vigens, dat honorem tota tibi gens.
Amplecti minimos magni solet esse viri mos.
Cor miseris flecte, quoniam probitas docet hec te.
Pauperie plenos solita pietate fove nos,
et transmontanos, vir transmontane, iuva nos.
Nulla mihi certe de vita spes nisi per te.
Frigore sive fame tollatur spiritus a me,
asperitas brume necat horriferumque gelu me,
continuam tussim pacior, tanquam tisicus sim.
Sencio per pulsum, quod non a morte procul sum.
Esse probant inopes nos corpore cum reliquo pes.
Unde verecundo vultu tibi verba precum do:
in tali veste non sto sine fronte penes te.
Liber ab interitu sis et memor esto mei tu.

A Hint To The Archbishop

All things have their time; as for me I crave but a moment,
Only the time to recite before you a handful of verses.
Here in your court, sacred prince, garments so slovenly make red
Cheeks full loath I can tell you with girlish blushes to mantle.
Hail to you, O Vastness, our realm's protection and fastness,
Whose views are long and well-planned, and enforced with a
    strong hand.
Rose of the Church, rosier priest never bore mitre and crosier,
Long live our Nestor, in the ship of state pulling the best oar.
Pious and just, question I have whether to make a suggestion,
Right sure 'twere treason to advise one so famed for his reason:
What would it make crumble if the great should cherish the
    humble?
Open to wretches your heart, since that is the way of the pure
    heart.
Let your hand save, or grant poverty's victims your favor;
You, a tramontane scion, are the help tramontaners rely on.
Small hope mine of living were it not for the chance of your
    giving.
Freezing and starvation have deprived me of all animation,
Winters with shivers fill me, till I know their bleakness will kill
    me.
Constantly I'm coughing, consumption is just in the offing;
Pulse-beats scarce existent are a warning that death is not distant.
Proof of my neediness is that my shoes are as poor as my dress is.
Hence as is most meet I importune you with words of entreaty:
Wearing such rags and tatters in your presence — believe me, it
    matters!
So may success greet you as in largess you're mindful of me too.

Estuans Intrinsecus

Estuans intrinsecus
ira vehementi
in amaritudine
loquor mee menti.
Factus de materia
levis elementi
folio sum similis,
de quo ludunt venti.

Cum sit enim proprium
viro sapienti
supra petram ponere
sedem fundamenti,
stultus ego comparor
fluvio labenti
sub eodem aere
nunquam permanenti.

Feror ego veluti
sine nauta navis,
ut per vias aeris
vaga fertur avis.
Non me tenent vincula,
non me tenet clavis,
quero mei similes
et adiungor pravis.

Mihi cordis gravitas
res videtur gravis,
iocus est amabilis
dulciorque favis.
Quicquid Venus imperat,
labor est suavis,
que nunquam in cordibus
habitat ignavis.

Via lata gradior
more iuventutis,
implico me viciis
immemor virtutis,

The Confession Of Golias

Indignation's fiery flood
   Scalds my inmost being;
I must chew a bitter cud,
   One conclusion seeing:
Light of substance is my blood,
   Restlessness decreeing,
So that down the wind I scud
   Like a dead leaf fleeing.

Let the wise man place his seat
   On the rock firm founded.
Hither, thither, I must beat
   By my follies hounded.
With the flowing stream I fleet,
   So my doom is sounded;
'Neath the arch of heaven my feet
   Nowhere yet have grounded.

Like a hapless ship I fare
   Left without a sailor,
Like a bird on ways of air,
   Some poor lost cloud-scaler;
Not a jot for chains I care,
   Nor for key nor jailer.
Sinful flesh is frail, I swear.
   Mine's the same — but frailer!

Dull and dour sobriety
   Never takes my money,
Give me loose society
   Where the jokes are funny;
Love will bring variety,
   Toil that's sweet as honey.
Pillars of propriety,
   Have you hearts as sunny?

Down the primrose path I post
   Straight to Satan's grotto,
Shunning virtue, doing most
   Things that I ought not to;

voluptatis avidus
magis quam salutis,
mortuus in anima
curam gero cutis.

Presul discretissime,
veniam te precor:
morte bona morior,
dulci nece necor,
meum pectus sauciat
puellarum decor,
et quas tactu nequeo,
saltem corde mechor.

Res est arduissima
vincere naturam,
in aspectu virginis
mentem esse puram;
iuvenes non possumus
legem sequi duram
leviumque corporum
non habere curam.

Quis in igne positus
igne non uratur?
Quis Papie demorans
castus habeatur,
ubi Venus digito
iuvenes venatur,
oculis illaqueat,
facie predatur?

Si ponas Ypolitum
hodie Papie,
non erit Ypolitus
in sequenti die:
Veneris in thalamos
ducunt omnes vie,
non est in tot turribus
turris Alethie.

Secundo redarguor
etiam de ludo,
sed cum ludus corpore
me dimittat nudo,

Little hope of heaven I boast,
   Charmed by pleasure's otto:
Since the soul is bound to roast
   Save the skin's my motto.

Hear me, prelate most discreet,
   For indulgence crying:
Deadly sin I find so sweet
   I'm in love with dying;
Every pretty girl I meet
   Sets my heart a-sighing:
Hands off! ah, but in conceit
   In her arms I'm lying.

Much too hard it is, I find,
   So to change my essence
As to keep a virgin mind
   In a virgin's presence.
Rigid laws can never bind
   Youth to acquiescence;
Light o' loves must seek their kind,
   Bodies take their pleasance.

Who that in a bonfire falls
   Is not scorched by flame there?
Who can leave Pavia's walls
   Pure as when he came there?
Venus' beckoning finger calls
   Youths with sportive aim there,
Eyes make captive willing thralls,
   Faces hunt for game there.

Give the chaste Hippolytus
   One day in Pavia,
He'll not long be virtuous;
   Next day you will see a
Lover most solicitous.
   Love's their one idea:
'Mid these towers so numerous
   Dwells no Alethea.

Next, I'm called in terms precise
   Monstrous fond of gaming;
Losing all my clothes at dice
   Gains me this worth naming:

frigidus exterius,
mentis estu sudo,
tunc versus et carmina
meliora cudo.

Tercio capitulo
memoro tabernam:
illam nullo tempore
sprevi neque spernam,
donec sanctos angelos
venientes cernam,
cantantes pro mortuis
"Requiem eternam."

Meum est propositum
in taberna mori:
vinum sit appositum
morientis ori,
ut dicant cum venerint
angelorum chori:
"Deus sit propitius
huic potatori!"

Poculis accenditur
animi lucerna,
cor inbutum nectare
volat ad superna.
Mihi sapit dulcius
vinum de taberna,
quam quod aqua miscuit
presulis pincerna.

Loca vitant publica
quidam poetarum
et secretas eligunt
sedes latebrarum:
student instant vigilant
nec laborant parum,
et vix tandem reddere
possunt opus clarum.

Ieiunant et abstinent
poetarum chori,
vitant rixas publicas
et tumultus fori,

While outside I'm cool as ice,
    Inwardly I'm flaming,
Then with daintiest device
    Poems and songs I'm framing.

Third, the tavern — here I dread
    Lies detraction's kernel:
Long on tavern joys I've fed,
    Never shall I spurn all
Till these eyes shall see instead
    Choirs from realms supernal
Chanting for the newly dead
    Requiem eternal.

My intention is to die
    In the tavern drinking;
Wine must be at hand, for I
    Want it when I'm sinking.
Angels when they come shall cry,
    At my frailties winking:
"Spare this drunkard, God, he's high,
    Absolutely stinking!"

Cups of wine illuminate
    Beacons of the spirit,
Draughts of nectar elevate
    Hearts to heaven, or near it.
Give me tavern liquor straight,
    Gouty lords may fear it —
Pah! their watered stuff I hate.
    Drawer, do you hear it?

Public life, there's no mistake,
    Certain poets find irking;
Courts they willingly forsake,
    In seclusion lurking;
There they study, drudge, and wake,
    No endeavor shirking,
Hoping one great poem to make
    Ere they cease from working.

Starveling rhymesters, when they thirst
    Water is their potion!
City din they count accurst
    And the crowd's commotion.

et ut opus faciant,
quod non possit mori,
moriuntur studio
subditi labori.

Unicuique proprium
dat natura munus.
Ego nunquam potui
scribere ieiunus,
me ieiunum vincere
posset puer unus.
Sitim et ieiunium
odi tanquam funus.

Unicuique proprium
dat natura donum:
ego versus faciens
bibo vinum bonum,
et quod habent purius
dolia cauponum,
tale vinum generat
copiam sermonum.

Tales versus facio,
quale vinum bibo,
nihil possum facere
nisi sumpto cibo;
nihil valent penitus
que ieiunus scribo,
Nasonem post calices
carmine preibo.

Mihi nunquam spiritus
poetrie datur,
nisi prius fuerit
venter bene satur;
dum in arce cerebri
Bachus dominatur,
in me Phebus irruit
et miranda fatur.

Ecce mee proditor
pravitatis fui,
de qua me redarguunt
servientes tui.

Foundlings by the Muses nursed,
 Fame's their only notion:
Fame they sometimes win, but first
 Die of their devotion.

Nature grants us each a prize,
 Fitly used, it waxes;
Mine in verse — not fasting — lies.
 Fasting so relaxes,
Any stripling half my size
 Bumps me off my axis.
Thirst and fasting I despise
 Worse than death and taxes.

One free gift from nature's stock
 Each man draws, and rightly;
Mine's for verse and getting chock
 Full of liquor nightly.
Broach the landlord's oldest crock
 Till I've mellowed slightly:
Good wine makes the fancies flock
 Copiously and brightly.

Let the verse be as the wine.
 Grasp this true technique well,
And like me, until·you dine,
 Neither write nor speak well.
Fasting, while I peak and pine,.
 Nothing comes in sequel;
Feast me, and these songs of mine
 Ovid could not equal.

Inspiration's wooed in vain,
 Fancy stays retired,
Till my craving guts obtain
 All they have desired;
Then let mighty Bacchus reign
 Till I'm duly fired,
Phoebus rushes to my brain —
 Lord, but I'm inspired!

Thus I stand condemned, but by
 My own accusation;
See, the courtiers prophesy
 My deserved damnation;

Sed eorum nullus est
accusator sui,
quamvis velint ludere
seculoque frui.

Iam nunc in presentia
presulis beati
secundum dominici
regulam mandati
mittat in me lapidem
neque parcat vati,
cuius non est animus
conscius peccati.

Sum locutus contra me,
quicquid de me novi,
et virus evomui,
quod tam diu fovi.
Vita vetus displicet,
mores placent novi;
homo videt faciem,
sed cor patet Iovi.

Iam virtutes diligo,
viciis irascor,
renovatus animo
spiritu renascor;
quasi modo genitus
novo lacte pascor,
ne sit meum amplius
vanitatis vas cor.

Electe Colonie,
parce penitenti,
fac misericordiam
veniam petenti,
et da penetenciam
culpam profitenti:
feram, quicquid iusseris,
animo libenti.

Parcit enim subditis
leo rex ferarum
et est erga subditos
immemor irarum.

Yet not one can testify,
  For his own salvation,
He is better armed than I
  'Gainst the world's temptation.

Even here before thy throne,
  Prince and true confessor,
Following the rule made known
  By our Intercessor,
Let him cast at me the stone,
  Be the bard's oppressor,
Who can swear that he alone
  Never was transgressor.

See, I've labored to record
  All my heart confesses;
Fulsome brews from pleasure's board —
  I spit out the messes!
Changed at last, I hasten toward
  This new life that blesses.
Man sees but the face; thou, Lord,
  Knowest the heart's recesses.

Now to virtue reconciled,
  Base desires I quiet,
Sweep and scour my sin-defiled
  Soul to purify it.
See me now a new-born child,
  New milk is my diet;
In my heart no more shall wild
  Vanities run riot.

Gracious prince, Cologne's elect
  Archbishop and warden,
Grant me mercy, nor reject
  One who sues for pardon.
Deign my penance to direct,
  Lest my heart should harden,
No commands will I neglect:
  Plant me in thy garden.

Pity me, thy suppliant,
  Let no thunder rumble.
Lion, king of beasts, doth grant
  Mercy to the humble.

Et vos idem facite,
principes terrarum:
quod caret dulcedine
nimis est amarum.

[Cum sit fama multiplex
de te divulgata,
veritati consonent
omnia prolata;
colorare stultum est
bene colorata,
et non decet aliquem
serere iam sata.

Raptus ergo specie
fame decurrentis
veni non inmodicum
verba dare ventis,
sed ut rorem gratie
de profundo mentis,
precepit ut dominus,
trahant offerentis.

Vide, si complaceat
tibi me tenere;
in scribendis litteris
certus sum valere,
et si forsan accidat
opus inminere,
vices in dictamine
potero supplere.

Hoc si recusaveris,
audi quod attendas:
paupertatis oneri
pie condescendas,
et ad penas hominis
huius depellendas
curam aliquatenus
muneris impendas.

Pater mi, sub brevi
multa comprehendi;
quia doctis decens est
modus hic loquendi;

O ye kings, were mercy scant
  Heaven itself would crumble.
Tasting bitters when they want
  Sweets will make men grumble.

[Thy renown is not concealed,
  Fame proclaims it shrilly,
And the many tales revealed
  Match the truth not illy.
Foolish would it be to wield
  Brush to paint the lily;
He who tries to sow a field
  Ready sown is silly.

Drawn by the reports I've heard
  I have come here lately,
Not to breathe some idle word
  Inconsiderately,
But my soul, as Christ averred,
  Feels most passionately
Grace on thee like dew conferred
  Should be reverenced greatly.

If it please thee, I would stand
  Here in humble station;
I could write thy letters, and
  Thus earn commendation,
Or if some great work were planned,
  That's my occupation:
Any style I can command,
  Deft at imitation.

Thou'lt refuse me, I forebode,
  Any trifling pension?
Yet dost ease the poor man's load
  Just by condescension.
All my sufferings I've showed,
  Claimed thy intervention,
And most kindly thou'st bestowed
  Statesmanlike attention!

Father mine, in little here
  Much is comprehended,
Hints that to a learned ear
  Tell what is intended.

et ut prorsus resecem
notam applaudendi,
non in verbo longius
placuit protendi.]

Hold me guiltless of a mere
    Hope to be commended:
There, I've said too much, I fear,
    So — my song is ended.]

Fama Tuba Dante Sonum

Fama tuba dante sonum,
excitata vox preconum
clamat viris regionum,
advenire virum bonum,
patrem pacis et patronum,
cui Vienna parat tronum.
Multitudo marchionum,
turba strepens istrionum
iam conformat tono tonum.
Genus omne balatronum
intrat ante diem nonum:
quisque sperat grande donum.
Ego caput fero pronum
tanquam frater sim latronum,
reus, inops racionum,
sensus egens et sermonum.

Nomen vatis vel personam
manifeste non exponam,
sed, quem fuga fecit Ionam,
per figuram satis bonam
Ione nomen ei ponam.

Lacrimarum fluit rivus,
quas effundo fugitivus
intra celum semivivus,
tuus quondam adoptivus.
Sed pluralis genitivus
nequam nimis et lascivus
mihi factus est nocivus.

Voluptate volens frui
conparabor brute sui
nec cum sancto sanctus fui.
Unde timens iram tui,
sicut Ionas dei sui,
fugam petens fuga rui.

Ionam deprehensam sorte,
reum tempestatis orte,

Jonah Come Again

Fame now bids the trumpet cry,
Heralds' voices raised on high
Summon folk from far and near;
Soon our best of men comes here,
Friend of peace and firm support,
At Vienne to hold his court.
Crowds from all the region round,
Mountebanks and rogues abound,
Minstrels mingle tune with tune,
Every sort of lewd buffoon
Before the ninth day joins the feast,
Hoping for windfalls at the least.
Yet I must hang my head in grief
As though my brother were a thief;
I've sinned, I fear, without excuse,
Hence words and wit are now no use.

A poet's dignities and name
It's plain to see I must not claim;
But, fleeing as Jonah fled of yore,
I have good right, by metaphor,
To bear the name that Jonah bore.

Tears in torrents once I shed,
An outcast whom you comforted —
Half living, I entered heaven the day
You took me for your protégé.
But my inveterate bawdy streak,
Fatal occasion, will too weak —
How dearly these have made me smart.

On fleshly joys I've set my heart;
Yes, I have wallowed with the swine,
The ways of saints have not been mine.
And so I feared your anger's rod
As Jonah feared the wrath of God,
Which to avoid I stopped for nought.

Jonah soon by fate was caught:
The sinner, when the storm grew high

condempnatum a cohorte
mox absorbent ceti porte.
Sic et ego dignus morte
prave vivens et distorte,
cuius carnes sunt absorte,
sed cor manet adhuc forte,
reus tibi.   Vereor te
miserturum mihi forte.

Ecce Ionas tuus plorat:
culpam suam non ignorat,
pro qua cetus eum vorat,
veniam vult et implorat,
ut a peste, qua laborat,
solvas eum, quem honorat
tremit colit et adorat.

Si remittas hunc reatum
et si ceto das mandatum,
cetus, cuius os est latum,
more suo dans hiatum
vomet vatem decalvatum
et ad portum destinatum
feret fame tenuatum,
ut sit rursus vates vatum
scribens opus tibi gratum.
Te divine mentis fatum
ad hoc iussit esse natum,
ut decore probitatum
et exemplis largitatum
reparares mundi statum.

Hunc reatum si remittas
inter enses et sagittas
tutus ibo, quo me mittas,
hederarum ferens vittas.

Non timebo Ninivitas
neque gentes infronitas;
vincam vita patrum vitas,
vitans ea, que tu vitas.
Poetrias inauditas
scribam tibi, si me ditas.

By the ship's crew condemned to die,
A whale engulfed with valvéd jaws.
I too deserve the death because
Nothing but evils I contrive,
Living in vice I cannot thrive.
Yet, deep within, my heart is strong:
To you, though sinning, I belong,
And haply you will pity me.

See now your Jonah on his knee
Beseeching you; he owns the sin
That caused the whale to suck him in,
Pardon he asks, and hopes to gain
Through you deliverance from the bane
That still engulfs him; he implores you,
Honors, dreads, cherishes, adores you.

If you revoke my penalty
And tame the whale by your decree,
The whale will in his fashion gape
And let the bald-head bard escape
Out of those jaws that spread so wide,
Where, famished, he is doomed to ride
Till he regain his destined port —
To be archpoet at your court,
Writing such things as please you well.
For reason's holy oracle
Bade you be born for this, express,
That by the grace of righteousness
And generous example you
Might this our fallen state renew.

My penalty if you revoke,
I'll fear no weapon's deadly stroke,
But where you send me, safe and sound
I'll go, my brows with ivy crowned.

The Ninevites I shall not fear,
Nor any stupid people here;
I'll live as holy men have done,
Shunning the things you bid me shun;
And poems more sweet than tongue can tell
I'll write you — if you pay me well.

Ut iam loquar manifeste:
paupertatis premor peste
stultus ego, qui penes te
nummis equis victu veste
dies omnes duxi feste,
nunc insanus plus Oreste
male vivens et moleste
trutannizans inhoneste
omne festum duco meste;
res non egit ista teste.

Pacis auctor, ultor litis,
esto vati tuo mitis
neque credas imperitis!
Genetivis iam sopitis
sanctior sum heremitis.
Quicquid in me malum scitis,
amputabo, si velitis;
ne nos apprehendat sitis,
ero palmes et tu vitis.

And now to make my meaning plain:
I'm crushed by poverty, the bane
Of foolish me, who in your house
Once held perpetual carouse
With money, horses, food, and dress.
Now like Orestes, mad no less,
Faring ill, by fears pursued,
Winning by tricks a little food,
With heavy heart I keep the feast.
You need no proof of that, at least.

Author of peace, stern magistrate,
Deal gently with your laureate,
Nor lend an ear to the unwise.
Now that my passion sleeping lies
No hermit could more holy be.
Whatever gives offense in me,
If you desire, I'll pluck it out.
But meanwhile, lest we die of drought,
I'll be the stake and you the vine —
With my support you furnish wine.

WALTER OF CHATILLON

GALTERUS DE INSULA, born at Lille about 1135, was never a wanderer like Primas nor a hanger-on at ecclesiastical courts like the Archpoet. He was a substantial churchman and humanist of no slight importance in his day. In the course of a varied career he was a student successively at Paris and under Stephen of Beauvais at Reims, head of a school at Laon, and canon of Reims. He held office for a time in the chancery of Henry II of England, and was thus enabled to become one of the congenial circle of John of Salisbury. The murder of Thomas à Becket shocked him into leaving the king's service. His poem denouncing Henry as a bloody tyrant was presumably written after he had reached the security of Châtillon, where for some years he followed the calling of a teacher. He next studied canon law at Bologna and visited the great court of Rome, only to observe with mounting indignation the venalities of high and low alike. In 1176 he returned to Reims to become the archbishop's secretary. He successfully completed on the subject of Alexander a formal epic which the world has succeeded in forgetting, and was rewarded by a canonry at Amiens. At the last he died horribly of leprosy, hastening his end by the severity of his penances.

Walter's *Alexandreid* reproducing Virgil at several removes is exactly the kind of poetry that one would expect a scholar and churchman to write. The surprising thing is that he did not confine himself to imitation of classical models but experimented in the new accentual rhymed stanzas of the secular poets. No doubt his songs, particularly the one on the birth of a love-child, belong in the category of literary exercises. They are undeniably lacking in spontaneity. Often the diction is stilted, the verse mechanical in a way that reminds us of the set perfection of crystals, not of the flexible beauty of organic things. Yet beneath the hard dry surface may be discerned the movement of a pawky, schoolmasterish wit which gives Walter's songs a faint but unmistakable originality.

It was as a satirist, however, that this poet made his deepest impression. He was an honest soul who could not be reconciled to the corruptions and hypocrisies of the world. With scholarly uprightness he inveighed against the rapacious princes of the church and the secular rulers who abetted them. He deplored the decay of learning and the smallness of the rewards bestowed on faithful and industrious students, emphasizing his points by ending each of his Goliardic quatrains with the "authority" of a line borrowed from Horace, Ovid, Lucan, or Juvenal. His fiercest blasts were reserved for simony. In his attacks on the greed of the clergy Walter attained a genuine intensity. The heavy words ran molten in the fire of his anger and were cast into great bronze bells to peal out God's judgments upon the unrighteous.

Importuna Veneri

Importuna Veneri
redit brume glacies,
redit equo celeri
Iovis intemperies:
cicatrice veteri
squalet mea facies:
amor est in pectore,
nullo frigens frigore.

Iam cutis contrahitur,
dum flammis exerceor;
nox insomnis agitur
et in die torqueor;
si sic diu vivitur,
graviora vereor:
amor est in pectore,
nullo frigens frigore.

Tu qui colla superum,
Cupido, suppeditas,
cur tuis me miserum
facibus sollicitas?
Non te fugat asperum
frigoris asperitas:
amor est in pectore,
nullo frigens frigore.

Elementa vicibus
qualitates pariant,
dum nunc pigrant nivibus,
nunc calorem variant;
sed mea singultibus
colla semper inhiant:
amor est in pectore,
nullo frigens frigore.

Love Laughs At Winter

Now wintry blasts have come again
    The toils of love impeding,
From swollen skies come sleet and rain
    Post haste to earthward speeding;
In token of the old campaign
    My cheeks are scarred and bleeding:
Such love is in my breast that I,
When winter is most frigid, fry.

While goose-flesh makes my skin grow tight,
    The fire within commences;
Sleepless I lie, night after night,
    And daylight racks my senses;
This life, too long continued, might
    Have serious consequences:
Such love is in my breast that I,
When winter is most frigid, fry.

O Cupid, when the gods divine
    Acknowledge their subdual,
Why pick a worthless heart like mine
    To serve your torch for fuel?
Even cruel cold does not incline
    Stern you to be less cruel:
Such love is in my breast that I,
When winter is most frigid, fry.

Variety of weather makes
    Our climate so enchanting,
In snow it cools, in sun it bakes,
    No temperature is wanting;
But hot or cold, for ladies' sakes
    My heart is always panting:
Such love is in my breast that I,
When winter is most frigid, fry.

Verna Redit Temperies

Verna redit temperies
prata depingens floribus,
telluris superficies
nostris arridet moribus,
quibus amor est requies,
cybus esurientibus.

Duo quasi contraria
miscent vires effectuum,
augendo seminaria
reddit natura mutuum,
ex discordi concordia
prodit fetura fetuum.

Letentur ergo ceteri
quibus Cupido faverit,
sed cum de plaga veteri
male michi contigerit,
vita solius miseri
amore quassa deperit.

Ille nefastus merito
dies vocari debuit,
qui sub nature debito
natam michi constituit,
dies, qui me tam subito
relativum instituit.

Cresce tamen, puellula,
patris futura baculus,
in senectute querula,
dum caligabit oculus,
mente ministrans sedula
plus proderis quam masculus.

On The Birth Of A Natural Daughter

The mildness of the spring returns
   When flowers in painted meads unclose,
And man on earth's new face discerns
   A smile of sympathy for those
Who see in love a restful thing,
A banquet for the famishing.

Two seeming contraries are met
   And mingle in one enterprise:
The more a man pays nature's debt
   The more his family grows in size,
A concord of opposing strains
Gives rise at last to bearing-pains.

Others may sing love's old sweet song,
   And doubtless Cupid grants them ease,
But when the dear plague known so long
   Revisits me and wrecks my peace,
Then I have reason to deplore
The love-life of a bachelor.

And specially to curse the day,
   That day when all my woe begins,
When following nature's mystic way
   I got a daughter for my sins;
Alas the day, how soon it would
See me confirmed in parenthood!

Yet thrive for father's sake, my lass,
   That you may be a staff to him
When in complaining age he has
   No other guide for eyes grown dim;
Tenderly mind him, little one,
And you'll prove better than a son.

Licet eger cum egrotis,
et ignotus cum ignotis,
fungar tamen vice cotis,
ius usurpans sacerdotis.
   Flete, Sion filie!
   Presides ecclesie
   imitantur hodie
   Christum a remotis.

Si privata degens vita
vel sacerdos vel levita
sibi dari vult petita,
hac incedit via trita:
   previa fit pactio
   Simonis officio,
   cui succedit datio,
   sic fit Giezita.

Iacet ordo clericalis
in respectu laicalis,
sponsa Christi fit mercalis,
generosa generalis;
   veneunt altaria,
   venit eucharistia,
   cum sit nugatoria
   gratia venalis.

Donum Dei non donatur,
nisi gratis conferatur;
quod qui vendit vel mercatur,
lepra Syri vulneratur.
   Quem sic ambit ambitus,
   idolorum servitus,
   templo sancti Spiritus
   non conpaginatur.

Si quis tenet hunc tenorem,
frustra dicit se pastorem,
nec se regit ut rectorem,
renum mersus in ardorem.

"Blind Mouths!"

Let me, though ill among the ill,
An unknown man among the unknown,
Make of myself the time's whetstone —
Unasked, a priestly office fill.
   Weep, daughters of Zion!
   The church's leaders
   Today seek Christus
     From afar.

If any man of mean estate,
Deacon or priest, would now obtain
A boon he long has hoped to gain,
A well-worn path leads to it straight:
   Make firm the agreement
   With Simon Magus,
   Then like Gehazi
     Take reward.

The clergy's state has fallen so low
The Bride of Christ is put to sale,
From generous sunk to general;
What reverence then can laymen show?
   Altars are at auction,
   The eucharist bartered;
   But grace is useless
     Bought and sold.

The gift of God is ever free,
Not to be granted otherwise;
Accurst is he who sells and buys,
Accurst with Syrian leprosy:
   Who eagerly worships
   The golden idol
   Knows not the Spirit's
     Pentecost.

If one by venal ways proceeds,
'Tis vain to attempt the pastoral role,
No rector can lack self-control
Nor be consumed by flaming greeds;

Hec est enim alia
sanguisuge filia,
quam venalis curia
duxit in uxorem.

In diebus iuventutis
timent annos senectutis,
ne fortuna destitutis
desit eis splendor cutis,
   et dum querunt medium,
   vergunt in contrarium;
   fallit enim vitium
   specie virtutis.

Ut iam loquar inamenum,
sanctum chrisma datur venum,
iuvenantur corda senum,
nec refrenant motus renum.
   Senes et decrepiti,
   quasi modo geniti,
   nectaris illiciti
   hauriunt venenum.

Ergo nemo vivit purus,
castitatis perit murus,
commendatur Epicurus,
nec spectatur moriturus.
   Grata sunt convivia;
   auro vel pecunia
   cuncta facit pervia
   pontifex futurus.

For greed, like another
Horseleech's daughter
The court corruptly
    Takes to wife.

In days of youth men fear decay,
Lest old age prove but Dead Sea fruit,
Lest fortune leave them destitute
And skin-deep beauty pass away.
    Then seeking for safety
    They run in danger,
    And give their vices
        Virtue's name.

And hence I speak it in disgust:
The holy oil is bought and sold,
And coltish longings fire the old
Whose hearts are never free from lust.
    Graybeards in their dotage
    Unwisely seeking
    Forbidden nectar
        Drink their bane.

Now shattered lies fair virtue's wall,
And no man lives whose ways are pure;
Praised is the name of Epicure,
And no one thinks of death at all.
    High feasts are in fashion,
    The future pontiff
    With gold and silver
        Paves his way.

Versa Est In Luctum

Versa est in luctum
cythara Waltheri,
non quia se ductum
extra gregem cleri
vel eiectum doleat,
aut abiecti lugeat
vilitatem morbi,
sed quia considerat,
quod finis accelerat
inprovisus orbi.

Libet intueri
iudices ecclesie,
quorum status hodie
peior est quam heri.

Umbra cum videmus
valles operiri,
proximo debemus
noctem experiri;
sed cum montes videris
et colles cum ceteris
rebus obscurari,
nec fallis nec falleris,
si mundo tunc asseris
noctem dominari.

Per convalles nota
laicos exleges,
notos turpi nota
principes et reges,
quos pari iudico
luxus et ambitio
quasi nox obscurat,
quos celestis ultio
bisacuto gladio
perdere maturat.

Restat, ut per montes
figurate notes
scripturarum fontes:
Christi sacerdotes

Minstrel's Farewell

The harp so often plucked by Walter's hand
    Now sounds an elegy,
Not that he mourns his self-exile or, banned
    From clerics' company,
    Bewails his leprosy:
  But that he sees the dreadful face
  Of doom for all of mortal race
Rushing upon this unsuspecting world apace.

Behold the Church's magistrates,
How fallen from their high estates!
  More lost and gone astray
  Today than yesterday.

We can but dread the coming on of night
    When deepening shadows crowd
In valleys low, but if the mountains' height,
    The hills, and all things proud
    Are covered by a shroud
  Impenetrable, we may claim
  (And none will hold our words to blame)
That night has seized upon the world and rules the same.

The figure points, as you must understand,
    To lay-folk lapsed from awe,
Kings sunk in shame, the "valleys" of our land,
    Princes with greedy paw
    Defiant of the law,
  Whose fame is dimmed by lusts abhorred:
  Yet still the vengeance of the Lord
Threatens to strike them down with heaven's twice-sharpened
    sword.

And as for mountains that should tower so high,
    What can we find more fit
Than priests of Christ, those wells that never dry,

colles dicti mystice,
eo quod in vertice
Sion constituti
mundo sunt pro speculo,
si legis oraculo
vellent non abuti.

Iubent nostri colles
dari cunctis fenum,
et preferri molles
sanctitati senum,
fit hereditarium
Dei sanctuarium,
et ad Christi dotes
preponuntur hodie
expertes scientie
presulum nepotes.

Si rem bene notes,
succedunt in vitium
et in beneficium
terreni nepotes.

Veniat in brevi,
Iesu bone Deus,
finis huius evi,
annus iubileus!
Moriar, ne videam
Antichristi frameam,
cuius precessores
iam non sani dogmatis
stant in monte crismatis
censuum censores.

Called "hills" in Holy Writ
And sanctified by it:
Their feet on Zion's top are based,
And they above the world are placed,
A glass of truth, if not by law's abuse defaced.

Our "hills" delight, in these degenerate days,
To pillage the unwary.
New customs now profane the ancient ways;
God's holy sanctuary
Is made hereditary;
Christ's portion feeds the parasite
And exile from true learning's light,
While prelates' minions gain rewards in heaven's despite.

The bishop's "nephews," mark and see,
Receive his offices in fee,
And with their lord's entailings
Inherit, too, his failings.

O good Lord Jesu, may the end be nigh!
Send us the promised year
Of jubilee, and quickly. I shall die,
Nor live to see the spear
Of Antichrist draw near;
Though now on sacramental ground
His vanguard stands, with creed unsound,
To levy in God's name tribute from all around.

Dum Galterus Egrotaret

Dum Galterus egrotaret
et egrotans cogitaret
quod ad vite terminum
vocaretur a potente,
metu mortis imminente
invocavit dominum.

Last Lines

Walter, on his sick-bed ailing,
Pondered while his strength was failing.
How man's powers are like a sword
Rendered up at life's conclusion;
Then he feared swift dissolution
And he called upon the Lord.

CARMINA BURANA: SATIRE AND MORALITY

About forty miles south of Munich, in the general direction of Oberammergau and Garmisch-Partenkirchen, lies the village of Benedictbeuern, the site of a monastery founded in 733. When the monasteries of Upper Bavaria were secularized in 1803, the contents of their libraries were removed to Munich. From Benedictbeuern came a late thirteenth century manuscript which had never been entered in the library catalogue, an under-the-counter book. It proved to be an anthology of poems, chiefly secular, some in German, but most in Latin. A majority of the latter were in the accentual, rhymed measures of the type written by wandering scholars. Along with a few religious plays and some prose pieces were poems of the most miscellaneous description: moral verses, satires, elegies on the fate of Troy, crusading hymns, laments on the instability of fortune. But the bulk of the collection was made up of love lyrics, nature poems, and drinking songs, and it is to these that the Benedictbeuern Songs or Carmina Burana owe their renown. Not all the poems are of German origin; some are demonstrably French, English, or even Italian, and sometimes better versions than those that reached the medieval collector are to be found elsewhere. But the collection as a whole is unrivaled.

The group that follows is no more than a token selection from the more than fifty serious poems that stand at the beginning of the anthology. It includes lively satires on the decay of learning, the vicious extortion of money by the clergy, and the widespread practice of simony. Then follow two moral poems on worldly vanity, a crusading hymn, and a short religious exclamation, the first stanza only of a poem reproaching prelates for their sinful lives. Two other pieces drawn from this section of the anthology are included later with the songs of the tavern and the open road.

Florebat Olim Studium

Florebat olim studium,
nunc vertitur in tedium;
iam scire diu viguit,
sed ludere prevaluit.
Iam pueris astutia
contingit ante tempora,
qui per malivolentiam
excludunt sapientiam.
Sed retro actis seculis
vix licuit discipulis
tandem nonagenarium
quiescere post studium.
At nunc decennes pueri
decusso iugo liberi
se nunc magistros iactitant,
ceci cecos precipitant,
implumes aves volitant,
brunelli chordas incitant,
boves in aula salitant,
stive precones militant.
In taberna Gregorius
iam disputat inglorius;
severitas Ieronymi
partem causatur obuli;
Augustinus de segete,
Benedictus de vegete
sunt colloquentes clanculo
et ad macellum sedulo.
Mariam gravat sessio,
nec Marthe placet actio;
iam Lie venter sterilis,
Rachel lippescit oculis.
Catonis iam rigiditas
convertitur ad ganeas,
et castitas Lucretie
turpi servit lascivie.
Quod prior etas respuit,
iam nunc latius claruit;
iam calidum in frigidum
et humidum in aridum,

These Times

Learning that flowered in days of yore
In these our times is thought a bore.
Once knowledge was a well to drink of;
Now having fun is all men think of.
Today mere striplings grow astute
Before their beards begin to shoot —
Striplings whose truant dispositions
Are deaf to wisdom's admonitions.
Yet it was true in ages past
No scholar paused from toil at last
Nor shrank from studies the most weighty
Till his years numbered more than eighty.
Now boys you'd think were barely ten
Throw off the yoke and pose as men,
Nay, even plume themselves as masters:
Blind lead the blind to swift disasters.
Our birds unfledged must now take wing,
Our donkeys tune the lyre and sing,
Bulls dance in hall, and heralds' calling
Is mocked by knaves at the plow-tail bawling.
Nowadays Saint Gregory in the snug
Argues, inglorious, with his jug;
Saint Jerome taxes all his rigor
To make his gains a farthing bigger.
Saint Augustine, when crops are fine,
Saint Benedict over casks of wine,
Hold many close confabulations
To gauge the market's variations.
Now Mary tires of sitting still,
While household cares make Martha ill;
Leah becomes a birth-controller,
And Rachel's eyes are bleared with dolor.
Cato, who seemed so strict of late,
In hot-spots learns to dissipate;
The chastity that was Lucrece's
In the mad whirl goes all to pieces.
Whate'er a former age despised
By modern lights is widely prized;
As into ashes sinks the fire,
As what was moist at length grows drier,

virtus migrat in vitium,
opus transit in otium;
nunc cuncte res a debita
exorbitantur semita.
Vir prudens hoc consideret,
cor mundet et exoneret,
ne frustra dicat "Domine!"
in ultimo examine;
quem iudex tunc arguerit,
appellare non poterit.

So virtue into vice is turned,
Toil is exchanged for ease unearned,
And all things, in a time disjointed,
Fall off and leave the ways appointed.
The wise man, pondering this apart,
Disburdens and makes clean his heart,
Lest crying "Lord! Lord!" he should stumble
When on the last day earth shall crumble;
For if the world's great judge arraign him,
No mortal power can then sustain him.

Manus Ferens Munera

Manus ferens munera
pium facit impium;
nummus iungit federa,
nummus dat consilium;
nummus lenit aspera,
nummus sedat prelium.
  Nummus in prelatis
  est pro iure satis;
  nummo locum datis
  vos, qui iudicatis.

Nummus ubi loquitur,
fit iuris confusio;
pauper retro pellitur,
quem defendit ratio,
sed dives attrahitur
pretiosus pretio.
  Hunc iudex adorat,
  facit, quod implorat;
  pro quo nummus orat,
  explet, quod laborat.

Nummus ubi predicat,
labitur iustitia,
et causam, que claudicat,
rectam facit curia,
pauperem diiudicat
veniens pecunia.
  Sic diiudicatur,
  a quo nichil datur;
  iure sic privatur,
  si nil offeratur.

Hec est causa curie,
quam daturus perfecit;
defectu pecunie
causa Codri defecit.
Tale fedus hodie
defedat et inficit
  nostros ablativos,
  qui absorbent vivos,
  moti per dativos
  movent genitivos.

"Sir Penny"

The hand that holds a heavy purse
Makes right of wrong, better of worse.
Sir Penny binds all bargains fast;
Rough is smooth when he has passed.
Who but Sir Penny settles wars?
He is the prince of counselors.
   Sir Penny's law no man can budge
     In courts ecclesiastic;
   Make room for Penny, ye who judge
     With consciences elastic.

Where Sir Penny's voice is heard
The sense of right is sadly blurred.
The poor man seldom finds redress
Whose one hope is his righteousness;
But pampered Dives needs no pull
Beyond the name of bountiful;
   Whate'er he asks, the judge concedes,
     And thanks his condescension.
   The man for whom Sir Penny pleads
     Makes good his whole intention.

While Penny vaunts, the wise man grieves
For justice fallen among thieves:
For courts that hear, to line their pockets,
The lamest suits that shame their dockets.
Wherever money's power is found
The poor man gets the run-around;
   The best of pleas is brushed aside
     That has no cash to back it,
   And lawful judgments are denied
     By those who own the racket.

Here's a case, let none deny it,
Fixed before the court can try it;
But when poor Codrus starts a suit,
Case dismissed — he's destitute;
Greed for money now disgraces
And infects grammatical cases:
   Our "takers away," the *ablative*,
     Rogues that deserve suppression,
   Prey on our *datives*, "those who give,"
     While *genitives* keep possession.

Sunt potentum digiti
trahentes pecuniam;
tali preda prediti
non dant gratis gratiam,
sed licet illiciti
censum censent veniam.
    Clericis non morum
    cura, sed nummorum,
    quorum nescit chorum
    chorus angelorum.

"Date, vobis dabitur":
talis est auctoritas,
danti pie loquitur
impiorum pietas;
sed adverse premitur
pauperum adversitas.
    Quo vult, ducit frena,
    cuius bursa plena;
    sancta dat crumena,
    sancta fit amena.

The fingers of the great, it's funny,
Are magnets for attracting money;
Whenever profits are in view
They put a price on all they do;
And further, risking retribution,
Assess a tax on absolution:
   Priests there are who think their cure
      Is less of souls than *soldi;*
   May angels ban that flock impure
      Whose holiness is mouldy.

"Give, and it shall be given you,"
So runs the precept old and true.
The piety of our wicked livers
Cries fervently for generous givers,
But not to help the poor, nor those
Who sink beneath their weight of woes.
   He whose purse with silver sags
      Laughs at bounds and measures;
   Holy are his money-bags,
      Holy be his pleasures.

Ecce Sonat In Aperto

Ecce sonat in aperto
vox clamantis in deserto.
In desertum nos deserti
iam de morte sumus certi.

Omnes quidem sumus rei,
nullus imitator dei,
nullus vult portare crucem,
nullus Christum sequi ducem.

Quis est verax, quis est bonus,
vel quis dei portat onus?
Ut in uno claudam plura,
mors exercet sua iura.

Iam mors regnat in prelatis,
nolunt sacrum dare gratis;
postquam sedent iam securi,
contradicunt sancto iuri.

Sunt latrones, non latores,
legis dei destructores,
Simon sedet inter eos,
multos facit esse reos.

Simon prefert malos bonis,
Simon totus est in donis,
Simon regnat apud austrum,
Simon frangit omne claustrum.

Simon aufert, Simon donat,
hunc expellit, hunc coronat,
hunc circumdat gravi peste,
illum nuptiali veste.

Si non datur, Simon stridet,
sed, si datur, Simon ridet,
iam se Simon non abscondit,
res permiscet et confundit.

Illi donat diadema,
qui nunc erat anathema:
iste Simon confundatur,
cui tantum posse datur.

Simon Magus

Hark, the voice of loud distress
Crying in the wilderness:
In life's deserts lost and lured,
Now of death are we assured.

Men are evil in behavior,
None will imitate our Savior;
Christ may bear his cross, who heeds?
None will follow where He leads.

Who is truthful, who is good,
Who would help God if he could?
Have at once your pennyworth:
Death now rules in all the earth.

Prelates own him lord and sire,
Putting sacraments to hire,
While secure in power they sit,
Making mock of Holy Writ.

Thus despoiling, not dispensing,
God they flout, His wrath incensing;
Simon Magus 'mongst them thrives,
Many ills that rogue contrives.

Bad men he prefers to good,
Loot is all his livelihood;
Through the South his power extends,
Every convent holds his friends.

Simon steals and Simon bribes,
Some promotes and some proscribes,
Schemes to cause a foe's miscarriage,
Plots a favorite's lucky marriage.

Simon howls unless he wins,
Grease his palm and Simon grins;
Trust him not to travel far
When there's aught to mix or mar.

See, the crown he places now
On a thrice accursed brow.
God confound that Simon Magus
Who is given such power to plague us.

Dum Iuventus Floruit

Dum iuventus floruit,
licuit et libuit
facere quod placuit,
iuxta voluntatem
currere, peragere
carnis voluptatem.

Amodo sic agere,
vivere tam libere,
talem vitam ducere,
viri vetat etas,
perimit et eximit
leges assuetas.

Etas illa monuit,
docuit, consuluit,
sic et etas annuit:
"Nichil est exclusum,
omnia cum venia
contulit ad usum."

Volo resipiscere,
linquere, corrigere
quod commisi temere,
deinceps intendam
seriis, pro vitiis
virtutes rependam.

Youth Departs

While the bloom of youth was fresh,
        Liberty and liking
Led us on in pleasant ways,
Inclination set the pace,
We could gratify the striking
        Hungers of the flesh.

Now the happy prospect dulls,
        Scope is duly scanted;
Age does not allow a man
Long to live on such a plan,
But the powers he takes for granted
        Limits and annuls.

Age rebukes our lustihood —
        Threatening, advising,
Offering some comfort yet:
"There is nothing to regret,
Thanks to God, the most surprising
        Lapses turn to good."

Let me waken from my dream,
        Leave my faults, amending
Deeds that I have rashly done.
Henceforth let my aim be one:
All my follies with unbending
        Virtue to redeem.

Iste Mundus

Iste mundus
furibundus
falsa prestat gaudia,
que defluunt
et decurrunt
ceu campi lilia.

Res mundana,
vita vana
vera tollit premia,
nam impellit
et submergit
animas in Tartara.

Quod videmus
vel tacemus
in presenti patria,
demittemus
vel perdemus
quasi quercus folia.

Res carnalis,
lex mortalis
valde transitoria,
frangit, transit
velut umbra,
que non est corporea.

Conteramus,
confringamus
carnis desideria,
ut cum iustis
et electis
celestia gaudia
gratulari
mereamur
per eterna secula.

This Dizzy World

This dizzy world
So madly whirled,
How false its joys and silly:
They take their flight
And vanish quite
As from the fields a lily.

This world's affairs
And mortal cares
A meet reward are earning,
For they impel
Our souls to hell
To sink in endless burning.

What gives delight
To touch or sight
In this our earthly pilgrimage
We must put by
Or else let fly
As oak trees shed their foliage.

All flesh is frail
And soon will fail,
Its rule is momentary;
'Twill pass or fade
Even as a shade
Unbodied, visionary.

Then quench we must
Our fleshly lust
By penance, prayer, and fasting,
That when we rise,
Our longing eyes
To heavenly joys upcasting,
We may rejoice
With heart and voice
Where life is everlasting.

Quod Spiritu David Precinuit

Quod spiritu David precinuit,
nunc exposuit
nobis Deus, et sic innotuit.
Sarracenus sepulcrum polluit,
quo recubuit,
qui pro nobis crucifixus fuit.
Quantum nobis in hoc condoluit,
quantum nobis propitius fuit,
dum sic voluit
mortem pati cruce, nec meruit!

    Exsurgat Deus!
    et dissipet hostes, quos habuit,
    postquam prebuit
    Sarracenis locum, quo iacuit.

Et adiuvet in hoc exercitu
quos signaverit
signo crucis, qua nos redemerit!
Iam venie tempus advenerit,
quo potuerit
se salvare, qui crucem ceperit.
Nunc videat quisque, quid fecerit,
quibus et quot Deum offenderit!
Quod si viderit
et se signet, his solutus erit.

    Exsurgat Deus!

Exsurrexit! et nos assurgere
ei propere
iam tenemur atque succurrere.
Ierusalem voluit perdere,
ut hoc opere
sic possemus culpas diluere.
Nam si vellet, hostes destuere
absque nobis et terram solvere
posset propere,
cum sibi nil possit resistere.

    Exsurgat Deus!

A Call to the Crusade

What David through the spirit once foretold,
God doth at length conclude;
The Saracens (so His purposes unfold)
With foul oppression hold
In bondage lewd
The holy Sepulchre where He was laid
Who for our sinful sakes was crucified:
A bitter price He paid
Who freely died
A death unmerited, suffering on the Rood!

God will arise, resistless in His splendor,
And crush the hostile host;
Though He permit the Sepulchre's surrender,
Let Saracens not boast.

And God shall aid His soldiers, those of us
Signed with the Holy Cross
And warranted by that sign miraculous.
He sends the valorous
Who take the Cross
For saving of their souls a time of grace:
Therefore let every man of us confess
His sins before God's face
And, ransomless,
Beg heaven's ransom in the sign o' the Cross.

God will arise!

Now Christ is risen, we rise up not in vain
His kingdom to begin;
Jerusalem is lost — His will is plain:
That we may hope to gain
Reprieve from sin
By warring till His foes be overthrown;
No need had He to grant us such a boon,
He might have fought alone
And conquered soon,
For none, opposing Christ, can hope to win.

God will arise!

Veritas Veritatum

Veritas veritatum,
via, vita, veritas,
per veritatis semitas
eliminans peccatum!
Te verbum incarnatum
clamant fides, spes, caritas,
tu prime pacis statum
reformas post reatum,
tu post carnis delicias
das gratias,
ut facias beatum.
O quam mira potentia,
quam regia vox principis,
cum egrotanti precipis:
"Surge, tolle grabatum"!

Truth Of Truths

Truth of truths, most true of all,
The way, the life, the truth, in one,
Making the path of truth to shun
Sin that would hold mankind in thrall.
Faith, hope, and love on Thee do call,
Word made flesh, O blessed Son.
Thou dost restore the original
Innocence lost in Adam's fall,
And dost, when earth's delights are done,
By grace alone
Our souls to blessedness recall.
O Miracle! what power is Thine!
O kingly Voice, that with divine
Majesty to the sick man said:
"Arise, take up thy bed."

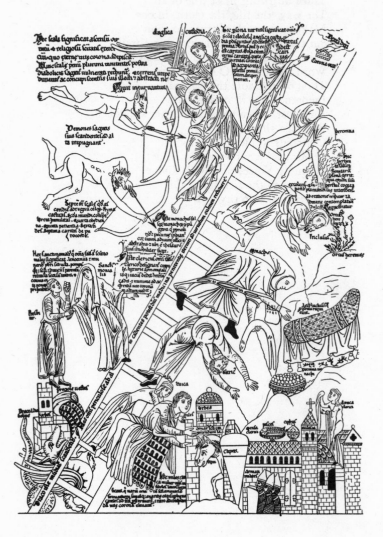

CARMINA BURANA: SPRINGTIME AND LOVE

The joy of spring, to us largely a literary convention, was a genuine experience to people of the Middle Ages, whether they lived in town or country, in monastery or shepherd's hut. The coming of the new year (in March) brought a rapture of deliverance. After four or five months of lowering skies, chill winds, dampness penetrating rooms, beds, clothes till even the brain seemed mouldy, discomfort at every turn and disease not unlikely, there would come a day when the sun shone again with golden promise, when it was possible to sit on the bench by the door without shivering, when the smell of the earth was sweet, and when musty houses could be thrown open to the air, purged of winter's filth, and freshly garnished.

> Thanne longen folk to goon on pilgrimages.

No wonder that young people walked in the fields and woods, that kisses and green gowns were given, and that everyone who could manage a few words of Latin uttered them in praise of springtime and love. It did not take much clergy to rhyme *amore* and *flore*.

Some of the many nature lyrics and love songs in the *Carmina Burana* were doubtless the work of clerics and may have formed part of the lighter repertory of wandering scholars and jongleurs of the church. But it is hardly possible that all these poems were made by learned men. Some of them are patently folk-songs in disguise or the near equivalent of the popular types of lyric soon to become common in the vernacular.

The love poems in the Goliardic tradition are invariably carnal. There is not a trace in these lyrics of the troubadour or courtly love convention. Woman was not conceived of as a far-away princess to be worshiped, but as an object of desire to be attained. Perhaps the lover is a young scholar and must weigh the claims of Mercury and Venus, but it is always the latter who carries the day. More often the lover is simply a predatory male and his Phyllis, Cecilia, or Juliana a charmer not unwilling to listen to his pleas. Or the lover may be a naive swain who does not know how to act in the time of the sweet sighs.

The rhetorical decoration of these poems is often drawn from classical mythology, with much reference to Juno and Jove, Apollo, Venus, Cupid, nymphs and satyrs, but the actual setting is more antique than the pagan world. It is pure immemorial nature. The urge of the mating season is implicit in these projections of poetic fancy and no other human considerations are permitted to interfere. The poems are no more accountable to morality than the flowing of the sap. That is why perhaps they are so perennially appealing to tastes somewhat jaded by a habit of looking before and after.

Ianus Annum Circinat

Ianus annum circinat,
ver estatem nuntiat,
calcat Phebus ungula,
dum in taurum flectitur,
arietis repagula.

Amor cuncta superat,
amor dura terebrat.

Procul sint iam tristia!
Dulcia gaudia
solempnizent omnia
Veneris gymnasia!
Decet iocundari
quos militare contigit
Dioneo lari.

Dum alumnus Palladis
Cytheree scolam
introissem, inter multas
bene cultas
vidi unam solam
facie Tyndaride
ac Veneris secundam,
plenum elegantie
et magis pudibundam.

Differentem omnibus
amo differenter.
Novus ignis in me furit,
et adurit
indeficienter.
Nulla magis nobilis,
habilis,
pulchra vel amabilis,
nulla minus mobilis,
instabilis,
infronita reperitur,
vel fide mutabilis.

Fealty To Venus

Janus rounds the year at full,
Spring announces summer's coming;
The sun's bright wain, with hot hoofs drumming,
Rolls in the region of the Bull
Beyond the Ram's domain.

Love conquers all — the proud, the fierce:
There is no mail Love cannot pierce.

Then put regrets away!
Sweet joys, we own your sway:
Venus keeps holiday
With all her pupils.
Mirth is the patrimony
Of those who serve Dione:
Then laugh and banish scruples.

While I still wore Wisdom's colors,
I was fain with Venus' scholars
At her school to make repair,
But of all the maidens there
Only one I saw was fair,
Featly formed, with Helen's features,
Most goddess-like of mortal creatures,
Full of charms that strike the eye,
But loveliest in her modesty.

Unique is my passion
For one so unique:
A fire of new fashion
That never turns ashen —
Its rage is not weak.
And where could one seek
A girl more magnanimous,
Free from all animus,
Lovely and lovable,
Full of docility
Joined to stability
Firm and immovable?

Eius letum vivere
est meum delectari;
diligi si merear,
hoc meum est beari.

Vincit amor omnia,
Regit amor omnia.

Parce, puer, puero!
Fave, Venus, tenero
ignem movens,
ignem fovens,
ne mori sit quod vixero,
nec sit Daphne Phebo
cui me ipsum dedo.

Olim tyro Palladis
nunc tuo iuri cedo.

To see her joys
Delights me best;
Were I her choice,
Then truly I'd be blest.

> *Love overcomes both great and small,*
> *Love rules, for Love is lord of all.*

Boy Cupid, spare a boy!
And, Venus, grant me joy:
Keep my fire
Mounting higher,
Let it not die, the flame I foster,
Nor let her prove a Daphne, over coy,
For me to love like Phoebus when I've lost her.

Once, long since, Wisdom was my god;
Now, Love, I yield, I kiss thy rod.

Amor Habet Superos

Amor habet superos;
Iovem habet Iuno.
Notus premens efferos
imperat Neptuno.
Pluto tenens inferos
mitis est hoc uno.

Amoris solamine
    virgino cum virgine.
Aro non in semine,
    pecco sine crimine.

Amor trahit teneros
molliori nexu:
rigidos et asperos
miro frangit flexu;
capitur rinosceros
virginis amplexu.

Virginis egregie
ignibus calesco
et eius cotidie
in amorem cresco;
sol est in meridie
nec ego tepesco.

Ludo cum Cecilia;
nihil timeatis,
sum quasi custodia
fragilis etatis,
nec marcescant lilia
sue castitatis.

Flos est; florem frangere
non est res secura.
Uvam sino crescere,
donec sit matura.
Spes me facit vivere
letum re ventura.

Love Robs The Cradle

Love controls the gods above:
  Jove takes Juno's orders;
South winds pressing waves with love
  Rule in Neptune's borders;
Love alone is master of
  Hell's relentless warders.

For joy of love with love I dally;
I love a maiden virginally:
Sweet is bloom without fruition,
And bliss that leads to no contrition.

Love in yielding natures born
  Very lightly presses.
Those who hold his power in scorn
  Feel his sterner stresses.
Lo, he tames the unicorn
  Through a maid's caresses.

Bright my flame and kindled soon;
  Fair the maid, none fairer.
Joys that keep our hearts in tune
  Day by day grow rarer.
Fervid as the sun at noon
  Glows the love I bear her.

When I play with Cecily
  Prudent fears are needless:
Of her young transparency
  Never am I heedless.
Lilies guard her purity —
  I would keep them weedless.

Such a flower as she, 'twould ill
  Serve my turn to break it.
I can leave the grape until
  Ripeness overtake it.
Thirst for happier issues still,
  May I live to slake it!

Gratus super omnia
ludus est puelle
et eius precordia
carent omni felle;
sunt, que prestat basia,
dulciora melle.

Ludo cum virginibus,
horreo corruptas,
et cum meretricibus,
semper odi nuptas,
nam in istis talibus
turpis est voluptas.

Quidquid agant alii,
virgo, sic agamus,
ut, quem decet fieri,
ludum faciamus.
Ambo sumus teneri:
tenere ludamus.

Volo tantum ludere,
id est: contemplari,
presens loqui, tangere,
tandem osculari;
quintum, quod est agere,
fuge suspicari.

Dalliance with the stronger sex
    Pleases girls completely.
Jealousies need not perplex
    Those that mingle sweetly,
Nor should any rancor vex
    Kisses given discreetly.

Simple girls I like whose lips
    Boast no false carnation.
Married women making slips
    Cause me no sensation;
I despise the kind that drips
    Cheap sophistication.

Never mind what others do,
    Girlie, since I say so,
Let me keep some awe of you,
    It is best to play so;
We are innocents, we two,
    And we mean to stay so.

All I want is that we should
    See each other's faces,
Speak, join hands, and when we would,
    Lightly give embraces,
And be just as good as good
    When I take you places.

Anni Novi Rediit Novitas

Anni novi rediit novitas,
hiemis cedit asperitas,
breves dies prolongantur,
elementa temperantur.
Subintrante Ianuario
mens estu languet vario,
propter puellam quam diligo.

Prudens est multumque formosa,
pulchrior lilio vel rosa,
gracili coartatur statura,
prestantior omni creatura,
placet plus Francie regina.
Mihi mors est iam vicina,
nisi sanet me flos de spina.

Venus me telo vulneravit
aureo, quod cor penetravit.
Cupido faces instillavit,
amor amorem superavit
iuvencule pro qua volo mori.
Non iungar cariori,
licet accrescat dolor dolori.

Illius captus sum amore,
cuius flos adhuc est in flore.
Dulcis fit labor in hoc labore,
osculum si sumat os ab ore.
Non tactu sanabor labiorum,
nisi cor unum fiat duorum
et idem velle. Vale, flos florum!

Salutation In March

The freshness of the new year comes once more,
  Winter's truculence ceases,
The days, though short, are longer than before,
  And the air's warmth increases.
Since the beginning of January
My hopes and fears like swirling tides vary,
So much I count one girl extraordinary.

She is discreet, and very fair of face,
  Shaming lilies and roses;
A frame compact of slenderness and grace
  This paragon discloses:
More than the Queen of France she can please me.
Sure, death grows neighborly and soon will seize me
Unless my Blossom of the Thorn will ease me.

Venus has wounded me with golden dart,
  My breast, see, it is bleeding!
Cupid with flaming torches fires my heart:
  New love old love exceeding,
All for her, the darling I would die for.
No dearer love than hers will I try for,
Although she give me pang on pang to sigh for.

I am made captive by my love of her
  Whose flower even now is blooming;
Sweet toil is mine with such a taskmaster —
  My lips gently presuming
To taste her lips, though kisses' healing powers
Will work no cure till these two hearts of ours,
Made one, shall wish the one thing . . . .
                    O my Flower of Flowers!

Letabundus Rediit

Letabundus rediit
avium concentus,
ver iocundum prodiit,
gaudeat iuventus,
nova ferens gaudia;
modo vernant omnia,
Phebus serenatur
redolens temperiem,
novo flore faciem
Flora renovatur.

Risu Iovis pellitur
torpor hiemalis,
altius extollitur
cursus estivalis
solis beneficio,
qui sublato bravio
recipit teporem.
Sic ad instar temporis
nostri Venus pectoris
reficit ardorem.

Estivant nunc Dryades,
colle sub umbroso
prodeunt Oreades
cetu glorioso,
Satyrorum concio
psallit cum tripudio
Tempe per amena;
his alludens concinit,
cum iocundi meminit
veris philomena.

Estas ab exilio
redit exoptata,
picto redit gremio
tellus purpurata,
miti cum susurrio
suo domicilio

Pipes Of Pan

The choir of birds is here again
   Elate in every feather,
New pleasure stirs the hearts of men
   In spring's jocund weather;
The sap is running in the boys,
All nature feels the season's joys:
   The sun serenely shining
With gentle rays has warmed the air,
And Flora, lest the earth go bare,
   Fresh coronals is twining.

Defeated by the smiling sky
   Is winter, man's benumber,
While day by day are flaunted high
   The banners of the summer,
Displayed in honor of the sun,
Who, in the glow of triumphs won,
   Is led to blaze the harder.
Meanwhile to give the time its dues
The goddess of sweet love renews
   Our half-forgotten ardor.

Now dryads haunt the summer woods,
   And where the slopes are shaded
Come forth the glorious sisterhoods
   Of mountain nymphs unjaded;
Through lovely Tempe satyrs tramp,
The pipes re-echo as they stamp
   The dance's merry measures;
The nightingale more sweetly sings
A descant to their caperings,
   Remembering springtime pleasures.

Summer comes back from banishment
   Entreated like a goddess,
And earth, with scarlet trim content,
   Resumes her colored bodice.
The little cricket fain would greet
The season from his snug retreat,

gryllus delectatur,
et canore, iubilo,
multiformi sibilo
nemus gloriatur.

Applaudamus igitur
rerum novitati.
Felix qui diligitur
voti compos grati,
dono letus Veneris,
cuius ara teneris
floribus odorat.
Miser e contrario,
qui sublato bravio
sine spe laborat.

A timid chirp he voices,
And soon with whistlings full of glee,
With song and shout and jubilee,
    All out-of-doors rejoices.

Then let us haste to celebrate
    The time of sweet renewing,
And count that man most fortunate
    Who prospers in his wooing;
Such blisses Venus grants to us
Her altar now is odorous
    With garlands fresh and jolly;
Far otherwise it is with him
Who toils long after hope grows dim —
    He takes the prize for folly.

Omittamus Studia

Omittamus studia,
dulce est desipere,
et carpamus dulcia
iuventutis tenere,
res est apta senectuti
seriis intendere.

Velox etas preterit
studio detenta.
Lascivire suggerit
tenera iuventa.

Ver etatis labitur,
hiemps nostra properat,
vita dampnum patitur,
cura carnem macerat,
sanguis aret, hebet pectus,
minuuntur gaudia,
nos deterret iam senectus
morborum familia.

Imitemur superos!
digna est sententia,
et amoris teneros
iam venantur otia;
voto nostro serviamus,
mos iste est iuvenum,
ad plateas descendamus
et choreas virginum.

Ibi que fit facilis
est videndi copia,
ibi fulget mobilis
membrorum lascivia,
dum puelle se movendo
gestibus lasciviunt,
asto videns, et videndo
me mihi subripiunt.

Philosopher's Holiday

Lay aside our studies,
It's well to be unwise,
Gather all the sweetness
Of youth as it flies;
Leave it to the old men
To ponder and advise . . . .

Swift age, it overtakes us
While study holds us down;
It's young blood that makes us
Frolic through the town.

When spring starts to fail us
Is winter far behind?
Bitter blows assail us,
Sorrows dull the mind,
The heart beats less quickly,
The hot blood chills,
And our joys yield to sickly
Age's brood of ills.

Live then like immortals!
Worthy is the aim:
To seek at love's portals
Heart's ease without blame.
Young likings are entrancing,
Why check them with a frown?
Outside the girls are dancing,
O hurry, hurry down!

What's here to see, I wonder?
The street's a carnival;
The dancers join and sunder,
Their arms flash and fall.
The willowy girls impress me,
So lithe as they speed;
I stand to watch, and bless me!
I from myself am freed.

Vacillantis Trutine

Vacillantis trutine
libramine
mens suspensa fluctuat
et estuat
in tumultus anxios,
dum se vertit et bipertit
motus in contrarios.

   O langueo!
   Causam languoris video
   nec caveo,
   videns et prudens pereo!

Me vacare studio
vult ratio.
Sed, dum amor alteram
vult operam,
in diversa rapior.
Ratione cum Dione
dimicante crucior.

Sicut in arbore
frons tremula, navicula
levis in equore,
dum caret anchore
subsidio, contrario
flatu concussa fluitat:
sic agitat,
sic turbine sollicitat
me dubio
hinc amor, inde ratio.

Sub libra pondero:
quid melius, et dubius
mecum delibero.
Nunc menti refero
delicias venereas,
que mea michi Florula
det oscula;
qui risus, que labellula,
que facies,
frons, naris aut cesaries.

In The Balance

My wavering mind resembles
The needle of the scales,
It hesitates and trembles
And tries to rest and fails;
Every casual blow
Redoubles its troubles:
It sways to and fro.

Heartsick am I!
And well I know the reason why.
No use to fly:
With open eyes, forewarned, I die.

"Go study," urges Reason.
I would obey indeed,
But when Love whispers treason,
Whose bidding should I heed?
While they pull me and shove,
I suffer, a buffer
'Twixt Reason and Love.

Like a bough ever tossing
When wind rocks the tree,
Like a pleasure-boat crossing
The wave-darkened sea,
When the anchor's to lack
And the sails are all riven —
    So shaken, so driven,
To stormy doubts given,
    I face the attack
Of Love pressing forward, while Reason holds back.

Now which is the better?
I weigh them and doubt,
And letter by letter
Try puzzling it out;
And my mind I beguile
With the thought of Love's blisses,
    My Florula's kisses,
And what a joy this is:
    To picture the while
Her face — hair and brow, then her lips, and her smile.

His invitat et irritat
amor me blandiciis.
Sed aliis
ratio sollicitat
et excitat me studiis.

Nam solari me scolari
cogitat exilio.
Sed, ratio,
procul abi! vinceris
sub Veneris imperio.

Love whets me and frets me
Such dainties he shows me,
    But Reason knows me
And straight to study sets me,
Ere Love can come between us.

Now one subdued to studious mood
Must pass his days in solitude —
    I cannot, though I try.
No thank you, Reason! Say goodbye!
You're vanquished by the might of Venus.

Lingua Mendax Et Dolosa

Lingua mendax et dolosa,
lingua procax, venenosa,
lingua digna detruncari,
et in igne concremari,

que me dicit deceptorem
et non fidum amatorem;
quam amabam dimisisse,
et ad alteram transisse.

Unde iuro Musas novem,
quodque maius est, per Iovem,
qui pro Danae sumpsit auri,
pro Europa formam tauri.

Sciat deus, sciant dei,
non sum reus huius rei,
sciant dei, sciat deus,
huius rei non sum reus.

Iuro Phebum, iuro Martem,
qui amoris sciunt artem,
iuro quoque te, Cupido,
arcum cuius reformido,

arcum iuro cum sagittis,
quas frequenter in me mittis,
sine fraude, sine dolo
fedus hoc servare volo.

Volo fedus observare,
et ad hec dicemus quare:
inter choros puellarum
nihil vidi tam preclarum.

Inter quas appares ita,
ut in auro margarita,
umeri, pectus et venter
sunt formata tam decenter.

Speaking For The Record

That lying and deceitful tongue,
So venomous, so loosely hung!
Fain would I pluck it out entire
And see it quite consumed by fire.

It said my love was counterfeit,
My bonds of faith not firmly knit,
My heart, like any infidel's,
Ready to turn to someone else.

Now all nine Muses I invoke,
And Jove, who knows love's puissant stroke —
Like gold he fell to Danae's arms,
In bull's form sought Europa's charms.

God knows, and all the gods know, I'm
Not guilty of that sort of crime;
The gods know, God knows, my intent —
Of that crime I am innocent.

I swear by Mars, and by Apollo —
Love's wiles they well know how to follow;
By thee too, Cupid, I make oath,
And by thy bow and arrows both,

That bow, those arrows which I dread,
So often have I seen them sped,
I swear, nor once equivocate,
I keep my troth inviolate.

My troth I gladly ratify.
And would you have me tell you why?
Because when maidens are on view
I've seen none lovelier than you.

You shine among them like a pearl
Set off by gold, a peerless girl:
Your form with all perfections graced —
Firm breasts, trim shoulders, slender waist.

Frons et gula, labra, mentum
dant amoris alimentum;
crines eius adamavi,
quoniam fuere flavi.

Ergo dum nox erit dies,
et dum labor erit quies,
et dum silva sine lignis,
et dum aqua erit ignis,

et dum mare sine velis,
et dum Parthus sine telis,
cara mihi semper eris;
nisi fallar, non falleris.

Your brow, your throat, your lips, your chin
Are each a prize for love to win;
Your hair it was first made me fond,
I can't resist a red-gold blonde.

And so till day breaks in the west,
Till labor is the same as rest,
Till forests without trees can thrive,
And fire and water cease to strive,

Till there are seas where sails are not,
And Parthians shoot no Parthian shot,
You'll be too dear for me to leave you,
Till I'm deceived, I'll not deceive you.

Sic Mea Fata Canendo Solor

Sic mea fata canendo solor,
ut nece proxima facit olor.
Roseus effugit ore color,
blandus inest meo cordi dolor.
Cura crescente,
labore vigente,
vigore labente,
miser morior.
Hei, morior, hei morior, hei morior!
dum quod amem cogor, sed non amor.

Si me dignetur quam desidero,
felicitate Iovem supero.
Nocte cum illa si dormiero,
si sua labra semel suxero,
mortem subire,
placenter obire,
vitamque finire
libens potero,
hei potero, hei potero, hei potero,
tanta si gaudia recepero.

Ubera cum animadverterem,
optavi manus, ut involverem,
simplicibus mammis ut alluderem.
Sic cogitando sensi Venerem,
sedit in ore
rosa cum pudore,
pulsatus amore,
quod os lamberem,
hei lamberem, hei lamberem, hei lamberem,
luxuriando per characterem.

Portrait Of Despair

Only by singing can I ease my fate,
As does the swan when death is nigh.
Time was my cheeks were roseate,
But tender grief has made their color fly.
> Troubles combining
> To add to my pining,
> And vigor declining,
> Prepare me to die:
Ho, to die, to die, to die,
Since I must love, but win no love thereby.

If she whom I desire would favor me,
The joys of heaven I'd gladly miss:
A single night with her to be,
For once to press on her ripe lips a kiss —
> Death could not fright me
> If then he should smite me,
> 'Twould only delight me
> To perish in bliss:
Ho, in bliss, in bliss, in bliss,
If I might know such ecstasy as this.

When I have thought of maiden breasts, what thrills
My questing hand would feel to press
In sport those unpreempted hills, —
Then seems her face like Venus' own, no less.
> Modesty, colder
> Than love, would withhold her,
> But love makes me bolder
> Her lips to caress:
Ho, caress, caress, caress,
And so exulting, drown in happiness.

O Comes Amoris

O comes amoris, dolor
cuius mala male solor,
   an habes remedium?
Urit amor me, nec mirum,
quia predilecta dirum
   evocat exitium,
cuius laus est singularis,
pro qua non curasset Paris
   Helene consortium.

Ergo solus solam amo
cuius captus sum ab hamo,
   nec vicem reciprocat:
quam enutrit vallis quedam,
quam ut paradisum credam,
   in qua pius collocat
hanc creator creaturam
vultu claram, mente puram,
   quam cor meum invocat.

Hec est vallis insignita,
vallis rosis redimita,
   vallis flos convallium:
inter valles vallis una,
quam collaudat sol et luna,
   dulcis cantus avium;
te collaudat philomena
vallis dulcis et amena,
   vallis dans solatium.

Sed quid queror me remotum
illi esse, que devotum
   me fastidit hominem?
Cuius nomen tam verendum,
quod nec mihi presumendum
   est ut eam nominem.
Ob quam causam mei mali
me frequenter vultu tali
   respicit, quo neminem!

Sally In Her Valley

What grief keeps company with love!
The torments I am weary of —
    Is there no means of curing?
Small wonder that I dread love's fire;
She plays the mischief, she is dire
    Whom most I find alluring,
Whose matchless beauty might eclipse
The face that launched a thousand ships
    And send Lord Paris touring.

I'm hers alone, would she were mine!
She plays me like a fish on line,
    No love to me returning.
Within a vale her dwelling lies,
To me it seems a paradise
    Fit for the Lord's sojourning.
He formed that radiant being there,
In spirit pure, in feature fair,
    For whom my heart is yearning.

This vale exceeds all vales beside,
A vaunted vale, the valleys' pride,
    Where rose-bloom veils each alley;
Available to birds, a vale
Where sun and moon themselves regale
    And longest love to dally;
The nightingales reveal thy worth,
Most valuable of vales on earth,
    O sweet and pleasant valley.

Yet why should I in grief demur
At being kept away from her
    Who scorns her faithful wooer?
Her very name, at last accounts,
I must not venture to pronounce
    Like one who really knew her.
It cost me her regard to try:
Such looks she gave me, as if I
    Were less than nothing to her!

Tempus Instat Floridum

Tempus instat floridum,
cantus crescit avium,
tellus dat solacium.
Eia, qualia
sunt amoris gaudia.

Huc usque, me miseram!
rem bene celaveram,
et amavi callide;
rea tandem patuit,
nam venter intumuit,
partus instat gravide.

Hinc mater me verberat,
hinc pater improperat,
ambo tractant aspere.
Sola domi sedeo,
egredi non audeo,
nec in palam ludere.

Cum foris egredior,
a cunctis inspicior,
quasi monstrum fuerim.
Cum vident hunc uterum,
alter pulsat alterum,
silent dum transierim.

Semper pulsant cubito,
me designant digito,
acsi mirum fuerim.
Nutibus me indicant,
dignam rogo iudicant,
quod semel peccaverim.

Quid percurram singula?
Ego sum in fabula,
et in ore omnium.
Hoc dolorem cumulat,
quod amicus exulat
propter illud paululum.

Flowering Time

The time draws near for flowers to spring,
Birds appear and sing and sing,
Earth now comforts everything.
Ah, my dear! well I see
Love has little joy for me.

Not to think of, not to tell —
For a while I hid my fear,
And I loved, I loved too well.
Now my fault must all be clear,
For I feel my body swell;
Childbed and its pangs are near.

For this my mother rates me,
For this my father hates me;
Both do their best to hurt me.
I sit at home outlawed,
I dare not stir abroad,
Nor anywhere divert me.

When in the street I venture out,
People stare that meet me
As if a monster walked about.
Each notes my shape, and judges;
One man another nudges,
And no one cares to greet me.

Nudging elbow so loose-jointed,
Finger always my way pointed,
Am I such a holy show?
Wagging head and curling lip,
Death's too good for me, *you* know,
Just because of one small slip.

Where shall I go, I alone,
I a byword now become
In the mouths of all and some?
What more can I know of grieving
Since my own true love is leaving
Till the storm be overblown?

Ob patris sevitiam
recessit in Franciam
a finibus ultimis.
Ex eo vim patior,
iam dolore morior,
semper sum in lacrimis.

From my father's countenance
He has fled to farthest France,
Leaving me alone to face
All the gibes, all the disgrace.
In despair I could die,
And I cry and cry and cry.

Exiit Diluculo

Exiit diluculo
rustica puella
cum grege, cum baculo,
cum lana novella.

Sunt in grege parvulo
ovis et asella,
vitula cum vitulo,
caper et capella.

Conspexit in cespite
scolarem sedere:
quid tu facis, domine,
veni mecum ludere.

A Thumbnail Pastoral

The farmer's daughter
    goes out at dawn
    with her flock,
    and wool to spin,
    and a staff.

In her flock are
    a sheep,
    an ass's colt,
    a billy-goat,
    a nanny-goat,
    a bull calf,
      and
    a heifer calf.

Hard she looks
    at the man of books,
    seated alone
    in a grassy spot:
"What are you doing there,
    studious sir?
    Come play with me —
    why not?"

Musa Venit Carmine

Musa venit carmine,
dulci modulamine:
pariter cantemus;
ecce virent omnia,
prata, rus et nemus,
mane garrit alaudula,
lupilulat et cornicula,
iubente natura
philomena queritur
antiqua de iactura.

Hirundo iam finsat,
cignus dulce trinsat
memorando fata,
cuculat et cuculus
per nemora vernata.

Pulchre cantant volucres,
nitet terre facies
vario colore,
et in partum solvitur
redolens odore.

Late pandit tilia
frondes, ramos, folia,
thymus est sub ea
viridi cum gramine,
in quo fit chorea.

Patet et in gramine
iocundo rivus murmure,
locus est festivus;
ventus cum temperie
susurrat tempestivus.

"This Lime-Tree Bower"

The Muse comes with song,
And ravishing division:
Let us too be singing,
For greenness is adorning
Meadows, farms, and parks;
Early in the morning,
Listen! the larks —
How their nestlings gabble!
And young rooks winging,
A raucous rabble;
While as nature urges,
The nightingale's dirges
Wail the ancient wrong.

Now the swallow trills,
The tuneful swan shrills
Mindful of its fate,
The cuckoo's cry fills
Woods with spring elate:
Honeyed are their bills.
Earth now is wearing
Her many-colored dress,
Lavish after bearing
She squanders spiciness.

The lime-tree wide around
Spreads its leafy mass,
Thyme grows under it
And a lawn of green grass
For country-dances fit.
There with joyous sound
Murmuring water flows:
A charmed spot to find,
When not too roughly blows
The seasonable wind.

Cedit, Hyems

Cedit, hyems, tua durities,
frigor abiit; rigor et glacies
brumalis et feritas, rabies,
torpor et improba segnities,
pallor et ira, dolor et macies.

Veris adest elegans acies,
clara nitet sine nube dies,
nocte micant Pliadum facies;
grata datur modo temperies,
temporis optima mollities.

Nunc, amor aureus, advenies,
indomitos tibi subjicies;
tendo manus; mihi quid facies?
quam dederas rogo concilies,
et dabitur saliens aries.

Pulchra mundi superficies
viridi gramine redolet,
induitur foliis abies,
picta canit volucrum series,
prata virent iuvenum requies.

Winter's End

Here, winter, here's an end of your severity.
Gone is the cold: stiffness and icy rigor;
Wind's wildness, dankness, and most bitter
Raging; all deadness and vile lack of vigor,
Wanness and fuming, aches and austerity.

Spring comes with delicate insinuation.
Clear shine the days without a cloud that's hateful;
By night the faces of the Pleiads glitter:
A tempering of the air ensues, a grateful
Seasonal softness and sweet relaxation.

Come, golden love, and bring with you prosperity.
Draw near; subdue all hearts yet unsubdued.
My hand in yours — what will you do to me?
A leaping ram I'll pledge in gratitude,
If she (your gift) will love me with sincerity.

The face of earth, so fair to admiration,
Perfumes itself with scents of June grass springing.
Even the evergreen fir-trees now look new to me,
The varicolored race of birds is singing,
And meadows bloom for young folk's recreation.

Omnia Sol Temperat

Omnia sol temperat
purus et subtilis,
nova mundo reserat
facies Aprilis,
ad amorem properat
animus erilis,
et iocundis imperat
deus puerilis.

Rerum tanta novitas
in sollemni vere
et veris auctoritas
iubet nos gaudere,
vias prebet solitas,
et in tuo vere
fides est et probitas
tuum retinere.

Ama me fideliter,
fidem meam nota,
de corde totaliter
et ex mente tota,
sum presentialiter
absens in remota;
quisquis amat taliter,
volvitur in rota.

The Faithful Heart

With pure and penetrating rays
   The sun warms all the earth,
The coming on of April days
   Confirms the world's rebirth.
Now quickly at love's bidding flames
   The heart of every boy,
And Cupid, boyish god, proclaims
   His empery of joy.

These glad renewings everywhere
   In honor of the spring
Summon us forth, dear love, to share
   The season's junketing;
Yet ways long known invite us too,
   And while your spring endures
Let faith and honor counsel you
   To hold fast what is yours.

So love me — love me faithfully,
   All truth in me you'll find,
A heart's entire fidelity
   With full consent of mind;
When far away I'm with you most,
   Such longings then I feel:
Whoever loves like this can boast
   He rides Ixion's wheel.

Ver Redit Optatum

Ver redit optatum
cum gaudio,
flore decoratum
purpureo,
aves edunt cantus
quam dulciter,
revirescit nemus,
cantus est amenus
totaliter.

Iuvenes ut flores
accipiant,
et se per odores
reficiant,
virgines assumant
alacriter,
et eant in prata
floribus ornata
communiter.

Spring, Etc.

Spring returns, the long awaited,
    Laugh, be glad!
Spring with blossoms decorated,
    Purple-clad.
Birds prolong their accords of song there
    How sweetly!
Trees renew their youth now,
Song brings joy in truth now,
    O completely.

While the youngsters welcome flowers
    New in bloom,
And refresh themselves with showers
    Of perfume,
Maidens meet them, in cadence greet them,
    So featly.
Through the fields they wander,
Flower-decked, growing fonder
    Indiscreetly.

Iamiam Rident Prata

Iamiam rident prata,
iamiam virgines
iocundantur, terre
ridet facies,
estas nunc apparuit,
ornatusque florum lete claruit.

Nemus revirescit,
frondent frutices,
hiems seva cessit:
leti iuvenes,
congaudete floribus,
amor allicit vos iam virginibus.

Ergo militemus
simul Veneri,
tristia vitemus
nos qui teneri;
visus et colloquia,
spes amorque trahant nos ad gaudia.

Green Pastures

Even now the meadows smile,
Now too the maids are glad,
The face of earth the while
  No more is sad.
Summer at last has shown her powers
And, gaily gleaming, donned her robe of flowers.

Again the woods are green,
The bushes are in leaf,
Winter's relentings mean
  The end of grief.
To girls in bud love leads the boys;
Rejoice, glad youngsters, with the flowers rejoice.

Then let us be employed
As Venus bids us be,
And, being young, avoid
  Despondency.
Our commerce is with lips and eyes,
While hope allures, and love bestows the prize.

Salve Ver Optatum

Salve ver optatum,
amantibus gratum,
gaudiorum
fax multorum,
florum incrementum;
multitudo florum
et color colorum
salvetote,
et estote
iocorum augmentum!
Dulcis avium concentus
sonat, gaudeat iuventus.
Hiems seva transiit,
nam lenis spirat ventus.

Tellus purpurata
floribus et prata
revirescunt,
umbre crescunt,
nemus redimitur;
lascivit natura
omnis creatura;
leto vultu,
claro cultu,
ardor investitur;
Venus subditos titillat,
dum nature nectar stillat,
sic ardor venereus
amantibus scintillat.

O quam felix hora
in qua tam decora
sumpsit vitam
sic politam,
amenam, iocundam!
O quam crines flavi!
In ea nil pravi
scio fore;
in amore
nescio secundam;

Young Man's Fancy

Spring, long missed, we greet you,
Lovers' hopes entreat you,
Joys that dwindle
You rekindle,
You engender bloom.
Flowers on every side
Variously dyed,
Welcome be you:
May we see you
Gayer tints assume.
Birds with pure melodious voices
Sound their carols, youth rejoices,
Blustering winter ebbs away,
The light wind stills its noises.

Pink is earth, the blossomer,
Greenness spreads like gossamer
Over meadows;
Dense are shadows
Where the groves are leaving.
Nature's frolic veins
Throb with growing pains.
Ardor graces
Radiant faces
Wonted vows receiving.
Venus now her folk will tickle,
Nectar-drops from nature trickle,
Sparks of longing fire the hearts
Of lovers true or fickle.

Happy fates agreeing
Brought my love to being —
She whose fairness,
Sweetness, rareness
Mark her absolute.
Hair like gold is hers,
Nought can I asperse,
She's perfection:
My selection
Brooks no substitute.

frons nimirum coronata,
supercilia nigrata
et ad Iris formulam
in fine recurvata.

Nivei candoris,
rosei ruboris
sunt maxille;
inter mille
par non est inventa.
Labia rotunda
atque rubicunda;
albi dentes
sunt nitentes;
in sermone lenta;
longe manus, longum latus,
guttur et totus ornatus
est cum diligentia
divina conpilatus.

Ardoris scintilla
devolvans ab illa,
quam pre totis
amo notis,
cor meum ignivit,
quod cor fit favilla.
Veneris ancilla
si non curat,
ardor durat,
moritur qui vivit.
Ergo fac, benigna Phyllis,
ut iocundar in tranquillis,
dum os ori iungitur
et pectora mamillis.

Like a crown her brow's attire is,
In her glance a smoldering fire is:
Eyebrows darkened, tips upcurved
To form the bow of Iris.

Cheeks of snowy whiteness
Tinged with rosy brightness —
These commend her
By a splendor
Rivals fail to reach.
Rounded lips that pout
Reddest rubies flout,
Lips her shining
Teeth enshrining, —
Slow to part in speech.
Slim is she, her fingers taper,
Long her throat and white as paper,
Formed as though with special care
The gods had sought to shape her.

Her allurements capture
All my heart with rapture:
I discover
How I love her
More than any wife.
Ah, my flame is fervent!
Venus, bid thy servant
Quench the burning
Of my yearning
Ere I lose my life.
Do, kind Phyllis, be my blessing:
Give me peace in love's possessing —
Eager mouth to eager mouth
And breast to bosom pressing.

Veris Dulcis In Tempore

Veris dulcis in tempore
florenti stat sub arbore
Juliana cum sorore.
  Dulcis amor!
Qui te caret hoc tempore
  fit vilior.

Ecce florescunt arbores,
lascive canunt volucres,
inde tepescunt virgines.
  Dulcis amor!

Ecce florescunt lilia,
et virginum dant agmina
summo deorum carmina.
  Dulcis amor!

Si tenerem quam capio
in nemore sub folio,
oscularer cum gaudio.
  Dulcis amor!

Juliana

Juliana, one sweet spring,
Stood with her sister, marveling
To see the fruit-trees blossoming.

Sweet love, sweet love!
To miss thee now would be a thing
Past thinking of.

See how bloom bursts from the tree,
And how the birds chant amorously;
So maidens melt in some degree.
Sweet love, sweet love!

See too the lilies, how they flower;
So maidens clustered in a bower
Sing the high god's resistless power:
Sweet love, sweet love!

Could I but hold in close embrace
That girl in some leaf-shadowed place,
Joy! What joy to kiss her face!
Sweet love, sweet love!

Dum Estas Inchoatur

Dum estas inchoatur
ameno tempore,
Phebusque dominatur
depulso frigore,

unius in amore
puelle vulneror
multimodo dolore,
per quem et atteror.

Ut mei misereatur,
ut me recipiat,
et declinetur ad me,
et ita desinat!

First Love

When summer was approaching
    And skies were blue and gold,
And, masterfully encroaching,
    The sun drove back the cold,

For one girl's favor longing,
    Then first my heart was torn,
And soon despairs came thronging
    To leave me pale and worn.

Would she have mercy on me,
    Would she be my friend,
And deign to look upon me —
    Then let the world end!

Vere dulci mediante,
non in Maio, paulo ante,
luce solis radiante
virgo vultu elegante
fronde stabat sub vernante
canens cum cicuta.

Illuc veni fato dante.
Nympha non est forme tante,
equipollens eius plante,
que me viso festinante
grege fugit cum balante
metu dissoluta.

Clamans tendit ad ovile,
hanc sequendo precor "Sile!
nihil timeas hostile."
Preces spernit et monile,
quod ostendi, tenet vile
virgo sic locuta:

"Munus vestrum," inquit, "nolo,
quia pleni estis dolo."
Et se sic defendit colo.
Comprehensam ieci solo,
clarior non est sub polo
vilibus induta.

Satis illi fuit grave,
mihi gratum et suave.
"Quid fecisti," inquit, "prave?
Ve ve mihi! tamen ave,
ne reveles ulli, cave,
ut sim domi tuta.

"Si senserit meus pater
vel Martinus maior frater,
erit mihi dies ater;
vel si sciret mea mater,
cum sit angue peior quater,
virgis sum tributa."

Something In The Pastourelle Line

Once when spring was in its heyday,
   Not in May — just short of May Day —
When the brilliant sunbeams shimmered in the glade,
   'Neath the branches growing greener
   Stood a maid of sweet demeanor,
On a shepherd's pipe the rustic creature played.

There I came, the day was fateful,
   For the nymph was far from hateful,
A poppet scarce above her crook in height;
   But no sooner was I heeded
   Than her bleating flock stampeded,
And she ran and bleated too in pretty fright.

So she neared the sheepfold, screeching,
   While I followed her beseeching:
"Hush, there's nothing to be scared of, on my honor."
   And I offered her a bangle
   If she'd try to see my angle,
But words and gift alike were lost upon her.

"I want no bracelet, stranger,"
   She said, "I knows my danger,"
And with her spindle tried to knock me down.
   Then we somehow fell to wrestling,
   And from struggling passed to nestling —
There was never lovelier queen in tattered gown.

Yet my pleasure and contentment
   Only deepened her resentment:
"You monster," she exclaimed, "what have you done?
   It's home I'd be! Goodbye, sir!
   O laws, I hopes you're wiser
Than to spill a word of this to any one.

"There's Pa, he'd whop me sartin,
   And my eldest brother Martin,
The day they finds it out, I'll mark with black;
   Or if Ma know'd, pity sakes!
   Ma, she's four times wuss'n snakes,
She'd use up a clump of birches on my back."

Laboris Remedium

Laboris remedium,
exulantis gaudium
mitigat exilium
virginis memoria:
unicum solatium
eius mihi gratia.

Nil proponens temere
diligebam tenere,
quam sciebam degere
sub etate tenera,
nil audens exigere
preter mentis federa.

In absentem ardeo,
Venus enim aureo
nectit cordis laqueo
corporis distantia,
merens tamen gaudeo
absentis presentia.

Iam etas invaluit,
iam amor incaluit,
iam virgo maturuit,
iam tumescunt ubera,
iam frustra complacuit
nisi fiant cetera.

Ergo iunctis mentibus
iungamur operibus,
mellitis amplexibus
fruamur cum gaudio:
flos pre cunctis floribus
colludemus serio.

Quam dulce, vi premere
mel, de favo sugere!
Quid hoc sit, exponere
tibi, virgo, cupio.
Non verbo sed opere
fiat expositio.

The Lover In Exile

Glad remembrance of my dear
Warms my exiled heart with cheer,
Even in thought to hold her near
Makes a home of foreign soil,
Dreaming of her graces here
Comforts me for all my toil.

Nothing rash would I propose:
So in tender youth I chose
One whom I might see unclose
Bud-like from her earliest days;
Though I dared not pluck my rose,
We grew fond in childlike ways.

Now I miss her more and more.
Love, whose golden chains we wore,
Binds us faster than before
While we languish far apart.
Even her lack I must adore,
Wistful blisses fill my heart.

Lo, the swiftly passing years
Leave my passion in arrears,
She has ripened, it appears,
As the fruits of summer swell;
All that she has been endears
What she still may be as well.

Soon our marriage of the mind
Must with actions be combined;
Each in other's arms entwined,
We shall revel in our luck:
What a flower of womankind
Waiting for my hand to pluck!

Then how sweet with deft address
Honey from the comb to press.
What I mean, lass, I confess
Some slight demonstration needs.
I'll expound our happiness
Not so much in words as deeds.

Tempus Est Iucundum

Tempus est iucundum,
o virgines,
modo congaudete,
vos iuvenes.

O. o. totus floreo,
iam amore virginali
totus ardeo,
novus novus amor
est, quo pereo.

Cantat philomena
sic dulciter
et modulans auditur;
intus caleo.

Flos est puellarum,
quam diligo,
et rosa rosarum,
quam sepe video.

Tua me confortat
promissio,
tua me deportat
negatio.

Tua mecum ludit
virginitas,
tua me detrudit
simplicitas.

Sile, philomena,
pro tempore,
surge, cantilena,
de pectore.

Tempore brumali
vir patiens,
animo vernali
lasciviens.

Veni, domicella,
cum gaudio,
veni, veni bella,
iam pereo.

Sweet Fire Within

The time is ripe for pleasure,
O maidens, leave your chores;
Come, squire them to the revels,
You lusty bachelors.

Sing O, sing O, as forth I go,
    From top to toe so blooming!
Fresh fires are all consuming:
A new, new love is dooming
    My total overthrow.

The nightingale, O listen!
Melodiously yearns,
And long the cadence echoes . . . .
The fire within me burns.

She is the flower of maidens
On whom my love is set,
A rose, a queen of roses;
Often our eyes have met.

Could I but win her promise,
There I could find content;
But should her lips refuse me,
O worse than banishment!

Her maiden charms entice me
To take my joy of her;
Her innocence forbids me
To make a toy of her.

O nightingale, be silent,
A moment stint your woe,
That my heart's canticle of love
May rise and overflow.

For winter now is ended,
The season grim and gray,
And the new zest of springtime
Disposes man to play.

Then, darling, come — have pity!
My joy — O grant it soon.
Come to me, come, my pretty,
For want of you I swoon.

Stetit Puella

Stetit puella rufa tunica;
siquis eam tetigit,
tunica crepuit.
Eia.

Stetit puella, tanquam rosula
facie splenduit,
et os eius floruit.
Eia.

"Whenas In Silks"

There stood a girl, in red she was gowned,
Her dress if you touched it made a
Swishing sound.
Eia!

Like a little rose-tree there she stood —
Her cheeks blown roses
And her mouth a bud.
Eia!

CARMINA BURANA: TAVERN AND OPEN ROAD

ANYONE may write the songs of spring, but Latin verses glorifying a wandering life or celebrating the joys of drinking, dicing, and drabbing must surely be the work of vagrom scholars, ribald priests, and renegade monks, the human detritus of the ecclesiastical and monastic establishments. Unsettled brain workers, *clerici vagi,* who used their idleness to no good purpose had become an increasing concern of church councils since the fifth century. The rise of universities only added to the floating population of educated men without employment, and confirmed their custom of drifting from place to place, begging for a living, singing scurrilous verses, and otherwise misbehaving themselves. By the beginning of the thirteenth century repeated canons directed against impostors, wandering scholars, and other ribalds, "joculatores seu goliardos," showed that restlessness had become the curse of Christendom. Goliardic jesters had to be restrained from interposing irreverent ejaculations during divine services, but nothing could curb their satiric ingenuity. In defiance of official displeasure they composed parodies of offices, prayers, and hymns, a Gamblers' Mass, a Paternoster of the Wine, a Gospel according to the Silver Marks. Living by their wits only stimulated them the more to extol the tavern and its pleasures, the excitements of the gaming table, and the satisfaction of the simple animal craving for food and women.

The second poem translated, *Exul ego clericus,* is a typical Goliardic address to a possible patron, with a blank space for the insertion of appropriate titles. *In taberna quando sumus,* for all its Breughel-like realism, manages to include lines that parody a hymn by St. Thomas Aquinas. The burlesque *Cum in orbem* giving the rules of the wandering order and the humorously formal *Denudata veritate* forbidding the mingling of water and wine show the irresponsible gaiety of the Goliard rhymster at its highest level.

Tempus Hoc Letitie

Tempus hoc letitie,
dies festus hodie:
omnes debent psallere
et cantilenas promere
et affectu pectoris
et toto gestu corporis,
et scolares maxime
qui festa colunt optime.

Stilus nam et tabule
sunt feriales epule,
et Nasonis carmina
vel aliorum pagina.
Quicquid agant alii,
iuvenes amemus,
et cum turba plurima
ludum celebremus.

Time For Gladness

Time for gladness, time for play,
Holiday we keep today:
Let the fiddle sound the strain,
Sing the good old songs again,
Hearts must beat in time with voices
Till the dancing blood rejoices;
Come, you scholars, most of all
Who best love a festival.

Pen and ink and copy-book,
How funereal they look;
Ovid's songs, how dull with age,
Still more any other's page.
Never mind what's not allowed,
Love is youth's temptation:
Here we go, a glorious crowd,
Hell-bent for vacation.

Exul Ego Clericus

Exul ego clericus
ad laborem natus
tribulor multociens
paupertati datus.

Litterarum studiis
vellem insudare,
nisi quod inopia
cogit me cessare.

Ille meus tenuis
nimis est amictus,
sepe frigus patior
calore relictus.

Interesse laudibus
non possum divinis,
nec misse nec vespere,
dum cantetur finis.

Decus (Herbipoleos)
dum sitis insigne,
postulo suffragia
de vobis iam digne.

Ergo mentem capite
similem Martini,
vestibus induite
corpus peregrini.

Ut vos deus transferat
ad regna polorum,
ibi dona conferat
vobis beatorum.

A Bidding Rhyme

I, a scholar far from home,
  Born to toil profess me,
Yet the clutch of poverty
  Sorely does distress me.

Learning is my joy, I would
  Eagerly receive it,
Were it not that want of means
  Forces me to leave it.

See, this cloak of mine is thin,
  Far too thin for wearing;
Many times I've felt the cold
  Chill my bones past bearing.

Chattering teeth when mass is sung
  Make me inattentive;
Vespers to a starving man
  Offer small incentive.

Honored Lord of (This or That),
  Friend of erudition,
Lend me such support as best
  Fits your high position.

Would you, as Saint Martin did,
  Keep your memory fragrant,
Bear in mind what pilgrims need,
  Clothe the tattered vagrant.

So may God prepare for you
  Everlasting station
Near the throne, and in good time
  Grant you his salvation.

In Taberna Quando Sumus

In taberna quando sumus,
non curamus quid sit humus,
sed ad ludum properamus,
cui semper insudamus;
quid agatur in taberna,
ubi nummus est pincerna,
hoc est opus ut queratur
sic quid loquar, audiatur.

Quidam ludunt, quidam bibunt,
quidam indiscrete vivunt;
sed in ludo qui morantur,
ex his quidam denudantur,
quidam ibi vestiuntur,
quidam saccis induuntur.
Ibi nullus timet mortem,
sed pro Bacho mittunt sortem:

Primo pro nummata vini;
ex hac bibunt libertini,
semel bibunt pro captivis,
post hec bibunt ter pro vivis,
quater pro Christianis cunctis,
quinquies pro fidelibus defunctis,
sexies pro sororibus vanis,
septies pro militibus silvanis.

Octies pro fratribus perversis,
nonies pro monachis dispersis,
decies pro navigantibus,
undecies pro discordantibus,
duodecies pro penitentibus,
tredecies pro iter agentibus.
Tam pro papa quam pro rege
bibunt omnes sine lege.

Bibit hera, bibit herus,
bibit miles, bibit clerus,
bibit ille, bibit illa,
bibit servus cum ancilla,

"Pastime With Good Company"

When we're at the tavern, we
Care not what this world may be,
But we set ourselves to dicing —
Sport of all sports most enticing.
Would you glance at our high jinks
Where one small coin pours out the drinks?
Would you have that scene unfurled?
Listen to me, I'll tell the world.

We play, we drink, 'tis thus, my friends,
We burn the candle at both ends.
Of those who most frequent the game
Some lose their shirts and mourn the same,
Some pile fresh garments on their backs,
Some hide their nakedness in sacks;
All thought of death each man postpones
When for the drinks we roll the bones.

First we throw a round to settle
Who shall pay, like men of mettle;
Next we drink to captives, then
Drink a third to living men;
Fourth, to Christians truly bred;
Fifth, to cheer the faithful dead;
Sixth, vain woman when she errs,
Seventh, Diana's foresters.

Eighth, to brothers born to roister;
Ninth, to monks that slip the cloister;
Tenth, to voyagers and sailors;
Eleventh, to discord-making railers;
Twelfth, to all who penance pay;
Thirteenth, to wanderers by the way;
And at the last to king and pope
We all inordinately tope.

Host and hostess, *he* drinks, *she* drinks,
Even the parson on a spree drinks,
The captain drinks, nor drinks alone,
The tapster drinks with greasy Joan.

bibit velox, bibit piger,
bibit albus, bibit niger,
bibit constans, bibit vagus,
bibit rudis, bibit magus.

Bibit pauper et egrotus,
bibit exul et ignotus,
bibit puer, bibit canus,
bibit presul et decanus,
bibit soror, bibit frater,
bibit anus, bibit mater,
bibit ista, bibit ille,
bibunt centum, bibunt mille.

Parum sexcente nummate
durant, cum immoderate
bibunt omnes sine meta,
quamvis bibant mente leta.
Sic nos rodunt omnes gentes,
et sic erimus egentes.
Qui nos rodunt confundantur
et cum iustis non scribantur.

They drink, they drink, a motley rout,
The stay-at-home, the gadabout,
The ignorant, the erudite,
The swift, the slow, the black, the white.

They drink, the poor man ill at ease,
The no-account gone overseas;
They drink, the boy, the reverend man,
Prelate and dean both clink the can.
They drink, the sister with the brother,
They drink, they drink, old maid and mother;
What hundreds, nay, what thousands, think!
Drink, drink, drink, drink, drink, drink, drink.

To quench their thirst what would avail
A hundred mugs of penny-ale,
When all are drinking without measure
And all in drinking find their pleasure?
Whoever treats these thirsty folk
By morning will be stony broke.
They sponge on us? We treat? Not much!
Good fellows, listen! *This is Dutch*.

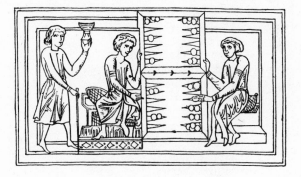

Bacche, Benevenies

Bacche, benevenies
gratus et optatus,
per quem noster animus
fit letificatus.

Istud vinum, bonum vinum,
vinum generosum
reddit virum curialem,
probum, animosum.

Iste scyphus concavus
de bono mero profluus,
si quis bibit sepius
satur fit et ebrius.

Hec sunt vasa regia,
quibus spoliatur
Ierusalem, et Babylon
regalis ditatur.

Ex hoc scypho conscii
bibent sui domini,
bibent sui socii,
bibent et amici.

Bachus forte superans
pectora virorum
in amorem concitat
animos eorum.

Bachus sepe visitans
mulierum genus
facit eas subditas
tibi, o tu Venus.

Bachus venas penetrans
calido liquore
facit eas igneas
Veneris ardore.

Homage To Bacchus

Welcome, Bacchus, hail, all hail!
    Loved and long desired;
God whose pleasures never fail,
    Let our hearts be fired.

Wine, wine, this very wine,
Generous wine and good,
Proves man's mettle, makes him shine,
Fosters brotherhood.

Raise the hollow cup aloft,
    Pour the liquor neat;
He who drains this beaker oft,
    He's a man complete.

Monarchs sacked Jerusalem
    Seeking bowls like this;
Babylon held no rarer gem
    For her kings to kiss.

Vassals pledge in cups of wine
    Fealty to the end;
Partners drink when they combine;
    Friend a health to friend.

When his might is manifest,
    Bacchus' mounting fires
Kindle in the manly breast
    Amorous desires.

Let the female of the species
    Not look disapproving:
When a woman's on a spree she's
    Much more kind and loving.

Bacchus, sending through her veins
    Warm and potent juices,
Melts her mood and she remains
    Apt for Venus' uses.

Bachus lenis leniens
curas et dolores
confert iocum, gaudia,
risus et amores.

Bachus, mentem femine
solet hic lenire,
cogit eam citius
viro consentire.

Aqua prorsus coitum
nequit impetrare,
Bachus illam facile
solet expugnare.

Bachus, numen faciens
hominem iocundum,
reddit eum pariter
doctum et facundum.

Bache, deus inclite,
omnes hic astantes
leti sumus munera
tua prelibantes.

Omnes tibi canimus
maxima preconia
te laudantes merito
tempora per omnia.

Gentle Bacchus soon removes
   Cares that follow after,
Gives us jests and joys and loves,
   Not forgetting laughter.

He makes female hearts incline
   Fondly on occasions,
Generous souls, soon touched by wine,
   Yield to men's persuasions.

Families rarely are begun
   Under a wet blanket.
Wine will get the business done
   Ere you think to thank it.

Bacchus, at whose jolly nod
   Bliss to man is sent,
Makes each toper seem a god,
   Wise and eloquent.

Bacchus, most illustrious,
   We thy devotees
Revel in thy gifts to us,
   Gifts that always please.

Loudly now we sing thy praise,
   See, our lungs are bursting:
Bacchus bless us all our days,
   Till there's no more thirsting.

Potatores Exquisiti

Potatores exquisiti,
licet sitis sine siti,
et bibatis expediti
et scyphorum inobliti,
scyphi crebro repetiti
non dormiant,
et sermones inauditi
prosiliant.

Qui potare non potestis,
ite procul ab his festis,
non est locus hic modestis.
. . . . .

Inter letos mos agrestis
modestie,
et est sue certus testis
ignavie.

Si quis latitat hic forte,
qui non curat vinum forte,
ostendantur ille porte,
exeat ab hac cohorte;
plus est nobis gravis morte,
si maneat,
si recedat a consorte,
tunc pereat.

Cum contingat te prestare,
ita bibas absque pare,
ut non possis pede stare,
neque recta verba dare,
sed sit tibi salutare
potissimum
semper vas evacuare
quam maximum.

Dea deo ne iungatur,
deam deus aspernatur,
nam qui Liber appellatur,
libertate gloriatur,

Topers All

Drinkers who revere your mission,
Connoisseurs of wine's condition,
Quenchless thirst be your ambition;
Cups in ceaseless repetition
May you quaff, with no contrition
    The morning after;
May your quips not breed suspicion,
    But endless laughter.

Where's the weakling quickly sated?
Here he won't be tolerated.
Feasts are meant for hearts elated,
Not the dour and sober-pated:
Sober among the illuminated —
    How *can* they bear it?
Villainy must be meditated,
    We all can swear it.

Any lad who's here detected
Shunning wine, or disaffected,
Let him forthwith be ejected,
Nor remain among the elected;
Better pack him off, neglected,
    Than wrongly cherish;
Should he fail us, as expected,
    Then let him perish.

When you drink for emulation,
Water not your pure potation;
Drink to shake the earth's foundation,
Drink to slur pronunciation,
Drink as if your soul's salvation
    On this depended:
To cause the swift evacuation
    Of jars up-ended.

God and goddess always bicker;
Wine scorns Water's flaccid ichor.
Liber (that's his name) is quicker,
Give him liberty, he'll trick her.

virtus eius adnullatur
in poculis,
et vinum debilitatur
in copulis.

Cum regina sit in mari,
dea potest appellari,
sed indigna tanto pari,
quem presumat osculari.
Nunquam Bachus adaquari
se voluit,
nec se Liber baptizari
sustinuit.

Joined with her, the god grows sicker
    In loathed communion.
Water shall not wed our liquor,
    We ban their union.

Let her pose as queen of ocean —
Goddess, if she likes the notion:
She'll not rouse our hearts' devotion
Mismatched with the stronger potion.
Ne'er by her, of his own motion,
    Was Bacchus lessened,
Nor with such presumptuous lotion
    Can he be christened.

Denudata veritate
succinctaque brevitate
ratione varia
dico, quod non copulari
debent, immo separari,
que sunt adversaria.

Cum in scypho reponuntur
vinum, aqua, coniunguntur,
at talis coniunctio
non est bona nec laudari
debet, immo noncupari
melius confusio.

Vinum sentit aquam secum,
dolens inquit: "Quis te mecum
ausus est coniungere?
Surge, exi, vade foras,
nec eodem loco moras
mecum debes facere.

"Vilis et inverecunda
rimas queris, ut immunda
mundi loca subeas;
super terram debes teri
et cum terra commisceri
ut in lutum transeas.

"Mensa per te non ornatur,
nullus homo fabulatur
in tui presentia,
sed qui prius est iocundus
ridens verboque facundus,
non rumpit silentia.

"Cum quis de te forte potat,
si sit sanus tunc egrotat,
conturbas precordia:
tonat venter, surgit ventus,
qui inclusus, non ademptus
multa dat supplicia.

The Debate Of Wine And Water

'Tis the naked truth, I warrant,
Two things mutually abhorrent
  Never should be joined in one;
Since the rule, most briefly stated,
Is to keep them separated,
  That should certainly be done.

When by any hand benighted
Wine and water are united,
  Then the wine-cup is abused;
Not a trace of real communion
Marks that base and praiseless union,
  'Tis confusion twice confused.

Wine, perceiving Water's closeness,
Crossly cries: "How dares your grossness
  Intermix itself with me?
Up, get out, be off, get moving,
This is not a place behooving
  Trash the like of you to be.

"Vile and shameless are you surely,
Slinking from the world obscurely
  Into holes and cracks you flood;
Or above ground, when you're trodden,
Earth combined with you grows sodden,
  So you change yourself to mud.

"Not by you are banquets brightened,
Not by you is converse lightened,
  All is silence when you come;
Fill with water the decanter
And the best of jokes and banter
  Die away and men are dumb.

"Water-drinking's an unfailing
Way to make a well man ailing;
  All his inwards go awry:
Bowels groan with wind insurgent,
Which, confined and not emergent,
  Causes many an anguished sigh.

"Sed cum venter est inflatus,
tunc diversos reddit flatus
ex utroque gutture;
et cum ita dispensatur
venter, aer perturbatur
a corrupto munere."

Aqua contra surgit ita:
"Turpis iacet tua vita
in magna miseria;
qui sunt tui potatores,
vitam perdunt atque mores
tendentes ad vitia.

"Tu scis linguas impedire,
titubando solet ire
tua sumens basia,
verba recte non discernens,
centum putat esse cernens
duo luminaria.

"Et qui tuus est amator
homicida, fornicator,
Davus, Geta, Birria;
tales tibi famulantur
tales de te gloriantur
tabernali curia.

"Propter tuam pravitatem
nullam habes libertatem
domos tenes parvulas;
sed ego magna sum mundo,
dissoluta me diffundo
per terre particulas.

"Potum dono sitienti,
ad salutem me querenti
valde necessaria;
quia veho peregrinos,
tam remotos quam vicinos,
ad celi palatia."

"Give the belly wind to vex it,
It will force through either exit
   Various blasts, both up and down;
Thus its tightness is corrected,
Though the atmosphere's infected
   With a gift of ill renown."

Water held the speaker blameful:
"You are he whose life is shameful,
   You the root of wretchedness;
They who find your cup delicious
Turn from virtuous ways to vicious,
   Plunge their lives in deep distress.

"You oblige the tongue to stammer
And confuse the laws of grammar,
   While the man who tastes your kiss
Reels and staggers, home returning,
Where if two small lights are burning,
   Full five score he sees amiss.

"Who are then your true admirers?
Base assassins and conspirers,
   Rogues and haunters of the stews,
Rascals they who live in riot,
Hoping still to profit by it,
   Such are all your tavern crews.

"Fearing evil, man deposits
All he has of you in closets,
   Keeps you under lock and key.
Through the world I'm free to travel,
Permeating soil and gravel
   Till the earth is soaked in me.

"Thirst I quench when lips are parching,
Pilgrims too I save from marching —
   Who can help them more than I?
Gliding on my tides, the palmer
Easier finds his way, and calmer,
   To the mansions of the sky."

Vinum hec: "Te plenam fraude
probas esse tali laude:
verum est quod suscipis
naves, post hoc intumescis,
dum frangantur non quiescis,
et sic eas decipis.

"Qui non potest te portare
et te totam desiccare
tendit ad pericula;
tibi credens, sic declinat;
ita per te peregrinat
ad eterna secula.

"Ego deus, et testatur
illud Naso, per me datur
cunctis sapientia:
cum non potant me magistri
sensu carent, et ministri
non frequentant studia.

"Non a falso potest verum
separare, qui me merum
non potare nititur:
claudus currit, cecus videt,
surdus audit, mens subridet,
per me mutus loquitur.

"Per me senex iuvenescit,
per me ruit et senescit
iuvenum lascivia:
per me mundus reparatur;
per te nunquam generatur
filius vel filia."

Aqua inquit: "Tu es deus!
per te iustus homo, reus;
malus, peior, pessimus:
facis verba semiplena
balbutire; cum lagena
sic fit sciens Didymus . . . .

Wine responded: "Your oration
Drips with guile and self-laudation;
    True, you're good at floating ships,
But you smash them when you're surly
Till with storm and hurly-burly
    They are little more than chips.

"Any man who cannot bear you,
Or by going dry forswear you,
    Finds his peril manifest;
He declines, and as you've stated,
He is soon by you translated
    To his everlasting rest.

"I'm a god, I would not say so
Were it not affirmed by Naso;
    Through me wisdom's given to all:
If professors did not tipple,
No applause would ever ripple
    Through the crowded lecture-hall.

"Truth from falsehood no contriving
Can divide unless the striving
    Start with many a goblet quaffed.
Lame men run without compunction,
Blind, deaf, dumb regain their function
    When I smile upon their draught.

"Age through me becomes more lusty,
Frolic youth more grave and trusty;
    I promote mankind's increase,
But no man inflamed by water
E'er begot a son or daughter;
    Left to you, the world might cease."

"You a god!" then Water answered,
"Thanks to you good men grow cancered —
    Bad, worse, worst — declining thus:
What men say you partly throttle
Till they babble; with his bottle
    Thus did knowing Didymus.

"Ego loquar veritatem:
dono terris ubertatem;
per me vernant omnia;
cum non pluit, exarescunt
herbe, fruges, et marcescunt
flores atque lilia.

"Mater tua tortuosa
nunquam surgit fructuosa,
sed omnino sterilis;
sua coma denudata
serpit humi desiccata,
vana atque fragilis.

"Fames terras comminatur
me cedente; perturbatur
deflens omnis populus;
pro me Christo christianus,
iudeus atque paganus
preces fundit sedulus."

Vinum ait: "[Tu] decanis
te collaudas verbis vanis;
alibi te vidimus:
universis cum sis nota
vilis et immunda tota;
credimus quod novimus.

"Tu fex rerum et sentina
que descendunt de latrina
suscipis, quod taceo;
sorde fetes, et venena
multa rapis, et effrena
que narrare nequeo."

Aqua surgit; se defendit
atque vinum reprehendit
de turpi colloquio:
"Quis vel qualis sit iam patet
iste deus, et non latet
tali vaticinio.

"Hear a truth that's most instructive:
Fields become through me productive,
  Everything is fresher made;
While if rain is scant, the tillage
Yields no harvest to the village,
  Flower and leaf, the lilies fade.

"Then the twisted vine, your mother,
Bears no fruit, nor could another;
  Barren all the vineyard stands;
Half denuded of her tresses
Closely to the ground she presses,
  Dry and stiff, with empty hands.

"Hunger stalks when I am lacking;
Drought will send the people packing
  Round the altars to complain,
There will Hebrew, Christian, pagan,
To Jehovah, Christ, or Dagon
  Pray incessantly for rain."

Wine replied: "You do keep harping
On your worth, and call me carping
  When another side I show;
Yet the whole wide world bears witness
To your vileness and unfitness:
  We believe but what we know.

"You absorb, by way of riddance,
Bilge from privies, drains, and middens,
  Many nameless filths as well,
Nasty droppings, waste, offscourings,
Poisonous drenches and outpourings
  More than I would care to tell."

Water rose to make rebuttal:
Wine, she said, was far from subtle
  So immodest was his speech:
"What you are your thought exposes
And your claim to godship closes;
  You're a pretty one to preach!

"Sermo tuus me non ledet;
tamen turpis male sedet
ore dei ratio:
ultra novem passus fere
nolo virus ne sufferre,
sed a me projicio."

Vinum ait: "Exornata
verba sunt post terga data;
non excludis vitium:
multi sepe te biberunt
qui per sordes perierunt,
per diei spatium."

Audiens hec, obstupescit
aqua; deflens obmutescit,
geminat suspiria.
Vinum clamat: "Quare taces?
Iam patet quod victa iaces,
rationis nescia."

Ego presens disputator,
huius cantus terminator,
omni dico populo
quod hec miscens execretur
et a Christo separetur
in eterno seculo.

"Though your libels fail to harm me,
Dirty talk might well alarm me
    Were the lips that spoke divine;
Faugh! your venom is your merit,
But I do not mean to bear it
    Even the length of paces nine."

Wine said: "Plain words have been spoken.
Dark suspicions they betoken,
    Which you have not yet denied:
Many men of you have drunken
Who in one day's space have sunken,
    Poisoned as by filth, and died."

Water, hearing this, astounded
Burst in tears and stood dumfounded,
    Heaving many a bitter sigh.
Wine exulted: "You're confuted?
Now at last your tongue is muted,
    Not a word can you reply."

I who wrought this disputation
Here, by way of termination,
    Say to people all and some:
Watering wine, if you abet it,
May Christ cause you to regret it
    Now and for all time to come.

Alte Clamat Epicurus

Alte clamat Epicurus:
venter satur est securus;
venter deus meus erit,
talem deum gula querit,
cuius templum est coquina
in qua redolent divina.

Ecce deus opportunus,
nullo tempore ieiunus,
ante cibum matutinum
ebrius eructat vinum,
cuius mensa et cratera
sunt beatitudo vera.

Cutis eius semper plena
velut uter et lagena;
iungit prandium cum cena,
unde pinguis rubet gena,
et si quando surgit vena,
fortior est quam catena.

Sic religionis cultus
in ventre movet tumultus:
rugit venter in agone,
vinum pugnat cum medone;
vita felix, otiosa
circa ventrem operosa.

Venter inquit: "Nihil curo
preter me; sic me procuro
ut in pace in id ipsum
molliter gerens me ipsum
super potum, super escam
dormiam et requiescam."

Belly-Worship

Epicurus loudly cries:
"A well-stuffed belly satisfies."
Belly's my god, and I his slave,
Such a god our palates crave,
With a kitchen for a shrine —
Ah, that incense is divine!

Here's a proper god at last.
No time is his time to fast;
Every morning ere he sups
He is belching in his cups,
And his liquor and his food
Are his true beatitude.

Lust for guzzling he indulges,
Like a leathern flask he bulges;
Lunch prolongs itself to dinner,
Hence his cheeks are never thinner
But are laced with many a vein.
Appetite is still his chain.

Strict religious exercise
Causes Belly's gorge to rise:
Inward qualms make Belly roar,
As when wine with mead makes war;
Life is happy, life is easy,
Just so Belly be not queasy.

Belly says: "I care for nought
Save myself; my only thought
Is to vegetate in quiet
Tending to my proper diet;
Give me but meat and drink, with those
Secure I sleep, serene repose."

Olim Latus Colueram

Olim latus colueram,
olim pulcher extiteram,
dum cignus ego fueram.

   Miser, miser,
   modo niger
   et ustus fortiter.

Girat, regirat furcifer,
propinat me nunc dapifer,
me rogus urit fortiter.

   Miser, miser.

Mallem in aquis vivere
nudo semper sub aere
quam in hoc mergi pipere.

   Miser, miser.

Eram nive candidior,
quavis ave formosior,
modo sum corvo nigrior.

   Miser, miser.

Nunc in scutella iaceo,
et volitare nequeo,
dentes frendentes video:

   Miser, miser.

Roast Swan Song

Aforetime, by the waters wan,
This lovely body I put on:
In life I was a stately swan.

Ah me! Ah me!
Now browned and basted thoroughly.

The cook now turns me round and turns me.
The hurrying waiter next concerns me,
But oh, this fire, how fierce it burns me!

Ah me! Ah me!

Would I might glide, my plumage fluffing,
On pools to feel the cool wind soughing,
Rather than burst with pepper-stuffing.

Ah me! Ah me!

Once I was whiter than the snow,
The fairest bird that earth could show;
Now I am blacker than the crow.

Ah me! Ah me!

Here I am dished upon the platter.
I cannot fly. Oh, what's the matter?
Lights flash, teeth clash — I fear the latter.

Ouch! . . . Ouch! . . .

Dum Caupona Verterem

Dum caupona verterem
vino debachatus,
secus templum Veneris
eram hospitatus;
solus ibam prospere
vestibus ornatus,
plenum ferens loculum
ad sinistrum latus.

Almi templi ianua
sevabatur plene,
ingredi non poteram
ut optavi bene;
intus erat sonitus
dulcis cantilene,
estimarent plurimi
quod essent Sirene.

Cum custode ianue
parum requievi;
erat virgo nobilis,
pulchra, statu brevi,
secundans colloquia
in sermone levi.
Tandem desiderium
intrandi explevi.

In ingressu ianue
sedens invitatus
ab hac pulchra virgine
sum interrogatus:
"Unde es, o iuvenis
huic applicatus?"
Cui dixi: "Domina,
vestri comitatus."

"Que est causa, dicito,
huc tui adventus?
qualis ad hec litora
appulit te ventus?"

The Temple Of Venus

Coming from the tavern once
  Reeling ripe with wine,
Happily I made a stand
  Just at Venus' shrine;
I was journeying alone,
  All my clothes were fine,
Full to bursting was my purse —
  What a chance was mine!

There I found the temple doors
  Not without a guard,
Slipping in as I had hoped
  Would, I saw, be hard;
Sounds of singing from within
  Sweetly filled the yard,
Such a song the Sirens sang,
  Mentioned by the bard.

More of her who kept the doors
  I might well repeat,
She was such a gracious girl,
  Pretty and petite,
Even the slightest persiflage
  From her lips was sweet;
So I told her my desire:
  "Open, I entreat."

Once within and at a loss
  Whom to interview
I was seated while my guard
  Questioned me anew:
"Whence are you, young man? To whom
  Is your coming due?"
Gallantly I answered her:
  "Lady, most to you."

"Nay, but truly, say what cause
  Brings you here, in sum.
What wind drives you to these shores?
  What town are you from?"

Dixi: "Necessario
venio detentus."
"Duxit te necessitas
et tua iuventus?"

"Intusque exterius
hasta vulneratus,
a sagitta Veneris,
ex quo fui natus,
telum fero pectoris
nondum medicatus,
cursu veni tacito,
quo sim liberatus.

"Incessanter rogo te,
virgo, te, beata,
ut hec verba Veneri
nuncies legata."
Ipsa mota precibus
fortiter rogata
nunciavit Veneri
verba destinata:

"Secretorum omnium
salus, o divina,
que es dulcis prepotens,
amoris regina,
egrum quendam iuvenem
tua medecina
procurare studeas,
obsecro, festina."

Iussu sacre Veneris
ductus in conclavi,
cernens eius speciem
fortiter expavi,
flexis tandem genibus
ipsam salutavi:
"Salve," dicens, "inclita
Venus, quam optavi."

"Quis es," inquit, "iuvenis,
qui tam bene faris?
Quid venisti, dicito,
quomodo vocaris?

"Necessarily constrained,"
  I replied, "I come."
"Ah, necessity and youth
  Gain the masterdom?"

"Venus, whose almighty power
  Caused my geniture,
Loosed an arrow from her bow,
  Swift it flew and sure,
Still the untended wound I bear,
  Grievous pangs endure,
Here I've come by secret ways
  Hoping for a cure.

"Noble damsel that you are,
  Hear me, I implore,
Be to Venus' sovereign ear
  My ambassador."
This I asked and pressingly
  Urged her more and more.
She, consenting to my prayers,
  Thus my message bore:

"Guardian of all mysteries,
  O my queen divine,
In whose all-compelling eyes
  Love and sweetness shine,
Let your quick solicitude
  Graciously incline
Toward this youth, who, sick at heart,
  Craves an anodyne."

Thanks to Venus' high commands
  All my hopes were crowned;
When I viewed her loveliness
  I was terror-bound;
Falling on my knees at length,
  These few words I found:
"Hail, O queen of heart's desire,
  Venus most renowned."

"Who are you, young man?" she said,
  "Courteously you speak.
What's your name? Say why you've come —
  What it is you seek.

Es tu forte iuvenis
ille dictus Paris,
ista de quo retulit?
Cur sic infirmaris?''

''Venus clementissima,
felix creatura,
cerno quod preterita
nescis ac futura.
Ipse sum miserrimus,
res iam peritura,
quem sanare poteris
tua levi cura.''

''Bene,'' inquit, ''veneris,
noster o dilecte
iuvenis, aptissime
sedes nostre recte!
Si tu das denarios
monete electe,
dabitur consilium
salutis perfecte.''

''Ecce,'' dixi, ''loculus
extat nummis plenus,
totum quippe tribuam
tibi, sacra Venus.
Si tu das consilium,
satis sum serenus,
tuum in perpetuum
venerabor genus.''

Ambo iunctis manibus
ivimus mature,
ubi stabant plurime
belle creature,
omnes erant similes,
unius nature
et unius habitus
atque vestiture.

Nobis propinquantibus
omnes surrexere,
quas ut salutavimus
responsum dedere:

Are you Paris, that young spark
  Fatal to the Greek —
He the oracle foretold?
  Why are you so weak?"

"Most benignant Venus, best
  Handiwork of God,
Past and future you confuse,
  What you say is odd.
I am but a wretched thing
  Soon to be a clod,
Yet you might restore my life
  Merely by a nod."

"Truly in good time you come,
  Dear young sir," said she.
"You have trusted in our care
  Most deservedly.
If you pay with lawful coin
  (Money down) our fee,
We will give our best advice,
  Healed you soon will be."

"Here," I told her, "take my purse
  Crammed with coins unspent;
Blessed Venus, all is yours,
  Given with free consent.
If you grant me your advice
  I shall be content
And will praise your godhead while
  Life to me is lent."

Arm in arm we then advanced
  Toward an inner room
Where were waiting in a band
  Many maids in bloom;
All were equal in degree
  Even as sisters, whom
You may find alike in mien,
  Dressed in one costume.

Soon as we drew near they all
  Hastened to arise,
And, when we had greeted them,
  Fashioned fit replies:

"Bene vos veneritis,
vultis hic sedere?"
Venus inquit, "Aliud
volumus explere."

Innuens his omnibus
dat abire cito,
pariter remansimus
in loco munito.
Solis quiescentibus
strato redimito
plura pertractavimus
sermone polito.

Exuit se vestibus
genitrix amoris,
carnes ut ostenderet
nivei decoris.
Sternens eam lectulo
fere decem horis
mitigavi rabiem
febrici doloris.

Postmodum transivimus
ire balneatum
in hortanum balneum
Iovi consecratum.
Huius aqua balnei
me sensi purgatum
omnibus languoribus
beneque piatum.

Ultra modum debilis
balneo afflictus
fame validissima
steteram astrictus;
versus contra Venerem,
quamvis derelictus,
dixi, "Vellem edere,
siquis inest victus."

Perdices et anseres
ducte sunt coquine,
plura volatilia,
grues et galline,

"Will it please you sit with us,
　Gladdening our eyes?"
"Nay," said Venus, "he and I
　Purpose otherwise."

Instantly the maids withdrew,
　Heeding her behest.
Thus we two were left alone,
　Snug as in a nest.
'Neath a single coverlet
　Soon we lay at rest,
Chatting long of dainty things
　Such as pleased us best.

Then the form of beauty's self
　Fully was revealed,
Snowy was her loveliness
　Like a cloud congealed.
Helped by her I sought the cure
　Only love can yield;
When my raging fever passed
　All my ills were healed.

Later to enjoy the bath
　Out of doors we hied
Where a garden swimming-pool
　Lay serene and wide;
Then in waters cool and deep
　It was sweet to glide.
All my languors disappeared,
　I was purified.

Coming from the bath, while yet
　Less than half renewed,
I was seized by hunger's pangs
　Not to be subdued;
So to Venus once again
　In distress I sued,
Saying: "I would like to eat,
　If there's any food."

Partridges and water-fowl
　Soon the table graced,
Cranes and hens and other birds
　Near at hand were placed;

pro placentis ductus est
modius farine:
preparatis omnibus
pransus sum festine.

Tribus, reor, mensibus
secum sum moratus,
plenum ferens loculum,
ubi vir ornatus
resedi; a Venere
sum nunc allevatus
nummis, atque sic ego
iam sum preparatus.

Terreat vos, iuvenes,
istud quod auditis:
dum sagittam Veneris
penes vos sentitis,
mei este memores;
vos quocumque itis,
liberi poteritis
esse, si velitis.

Cakes were brought of wheaten flour
    Stirred into a paste;
When the meal was all prepared,
    Then I dined in haste.

Full three months, I well believe,
    I remained fast hooked.
Since I brought a heavy purse,
    Like a lord I looked,
And my lordship lasted till —
    Absolutely rooked —
Venus turned me out of doors.
    Now my goose is cooked.

Take fair warning, all young men,
    You that hear my fate:
Soon as Venus' arrow flies
    Think of my estate,
Then upon your coming woes
    Pause and meditate.
If you flee you may get free
    Ere it be too late.

O Fortuna

O Fortuna,
velut luna
statu variabilis,
semper crescis
aut decrescis;
vita detestabilis
nunc obdurat
et tunc curat
ludo mentis aciem,
egestatem,
potestatem
dissolvit ut glaciem.

Sors inmanis
et inanis,
rota tu volubilis,
status malus,
vana salus
semper dissolubilis,
obumbratam
et velatam
mihi quoque niteris,
nunc per ludum
dorsum nudum
fero tui sceleris.

Sors salutis
et virtutis
mihi nunc contraria,
est affectus
et defectus
semper in angaria;
hac in hora
sine mora
cordis pulsum tangite,
quod per sortem
sternit fortem
mecum omnes plangite.

Soldier Of Fortune

O Fortune, most contrary,
Of changing never chary,
    Now small, now great,
    Appears your state;
Just like the moon you vary.

The life your servants suffer
Makes wits grow sharper, tougher,
    Through games of chance
    Which much enhance
Both easy times and rougher.

Lo, penury or power
May greet us any hour:
    Your wheel revolves
    And all dissolves
Like ice beneath a shower.

O Lady Luck, alluring
But faithless in securing
    The wealth we prize,
    From me likewise
You hide, your face obscuring.

I've bet my shirt and lost,
My hopes of bliss are crossed;
    And, lose or gain,
    I still remain
Hard up — but hang the cost!

My pounding pulses crave
One smile for me, your slave . . . .
    Friends, keep with me
    And weep with me:
She favors *not* the brave.

Si Quis Deciorum

Si quis Deciorum
dives officio
gaudes in Vagorum
esse consortio,
vina nunquam spernas,
diligas tabernas.

Bachi, qui est spiritus, infusio
gentes allicit bibendi studio,
curarumque tedium
solvit, et dat gaudium.

Terminum nullum teneat nostra concio,
bibat funditus confisa Decio,
nam ferre scimus eum
Fortune clypeum.

Circa frequens studium sis sedula,
apta digitos gens, eris emula
ad fraudem Decii
sub spe stipendii.

Qui perdit pallium
scit esse Decium
fortune nuntium
sibi non prospere,
dum ludit temere
gratis volens bibere.

Lusorum studia
sunt fraudis conscia;
perdentis tedia
sunt illi gaudium,
qui tenet pallium
per fraudis vitium.

Ne miretur homo talis,
quem tus, es nudavit,
nam sors item cogit talis
dare penam factis malis,
Iovemque beavit.

Decius, God Of Dice

If you among the Decians
In fortune's smiles are basking,
The fellowship of vagrant clerks
Is yours for the asking;
Granting you've no distaste for wines,
Seek out the taverns by their signs.

Bacchus, who is a spirit, draws
All sorts of men to own his laws;
Devoted sots he frees from cares,
He gives what joys are theirs.

Take us: our party never ends,
We drink whatever Decius sends;
We know what power the god must wield
Who bears Fortuna's shield.

Keep practicing, ye folk of nimble fingers,
No one can win at dicing who malingers.
All frauds of Decius, try them
In hope to profit by them.

The man whose cloak's imperiled
Knows Decius is no herald
Of lucky chance for him;
He sees his hopes grow dim,
Yet recklessly keeps throwing
While free drinks still are flowing.

The gamblers' god
Is simply Fraud;
The pang of losses
One counts a joke
When double-crosses
Win him a cloak.

Let no man blame the bitchéd bones
Whom *deuce-ace* strips of all he owns;
An even-handed Fate, pursuing,
Makes dice atone for their misdoing, —
And he has blessed God.

Ut plus ludat
quem sors nudat
lucri spes hortatur;
sed dum testes
trahunt vestes,
non auxiliatur.

In taberna
fraus eterna
semper est in ludo,
hanc qui amat
sepe clamat
sedens dorso nudo:

"Ve tuis donis, Decie,
tibi fraus et insidie;
turbam facis ludentium
paris stridorem dentium,
lusorum enim studia
sunt fraudes et rapina,
que mihi supplicium
merso dant in ruina.

"Fortune bona primitus
voluntas est inmersa,
in meque mihi penitus
novercatur aversa.
In valle hec parapsidis
stat fronte capillata,
que nunc aures aspidis
habet retro calvata."

Schuch! clamat nudus in frigore,
cui gelu riget in pectore,
quem tremor angit nudo corpore,
dum optat, ut sedeat
estatis tempore
sub arbore.

Per Decium
supplicium

One plays the more
In hope to score
When fortune leaves him bare,
Yet pawning clothes
To back one's throws
May not prevent despair.

Who can gainsay
That tavern play
Will always smell of guile?
With back unclad
And aspect sad
The victim mourns the while:

"Specious are your gifts, O Decius,
Fraud and ruin lurk beneath;
Thanks to you this crowd of gamesters
Fare alike with chattering teeth.
Gamblers with the snares they weave
Seek to pillage and deceive;
Ah, what pains the villains cause me!
Now I'm sunk, my ruin awes me.

"Hidden fortune comes unbidden.
No good will has Luck for me,
Like a mother-in-law her dealings
Show her harsh as harsh can be.
In the dice-cup's bowl she stands,
Her forelock streaming toward our hands,
We clutch, we call to her, and find
The jade is deaf and bald behind."

Ker-*chew!* exclaims a naked one
Who miserably cowers
While shivers through his body run;
Of summertime he dreams, when he
Can sit for hours
Under a tree.

If Decius
Grows capricious,

suis datur cultoribus,
quos seviens
urget hyems
semper suis temporibus.

Sub digito
sollicito
latet fraus et deceptio,
unde oritur,
dum luditur,
sepe litis dissensio.

Deceptoris est mos,
veloces et tardos
et graves fraudet sors;
sint secum Decii,
sed furti conscii,
dum ludunt socii.

Sub quorum studio
fraus et deceptio
regnant cum Decio
non equis legibus,
damnandus animus,
sed innexis retibus.

Corde si quis tam devoto
ludum imitatur,
huius rei testis Otto,
colum cuius regit Clotho,
quod sepe nudatur.

Causa ludi
sepe nudi
sunt mei consortes;
dum sibi prestem,
super vestem
meam mittunt sortes.

Heu, pro ludo
sepe nudo
dat vestem saccus,

His followers must suffer;
And blowing
Winter, snowing,
Makes going all the rougher.

Deception hides
And fraud abides
Where fingers have no morals;
When tricks are played
The game is made
A cause of strife and quarrels.

The cheat is wont to argue thus:
Luck still betrays the impetuous,
Likewise the slow and heavy-handed;
Let Decians be together banded —
Be with the thief confederated
When partners for the game are mated.

Thus they endeavor
That justice never
Shall rule in their affairs;
Fair play's outmoded,
A myth exploded —
Decius loves snares in snares.

If one whose heart is void of shame
Should try to imitate our game,
(Otto be witness of the same)
May Clotho wield her spindle
So that his garments dwindle.

It irritates
My gambling mates
To pawn their clothes for payment,
When I am dressed
By far the best
They cast lots for *my* raiment.

Woe's me, that sacks
Should warm their backs
Who set the dice a-rolling,

sed dum penas
mortis venas
dat nescire Bacchus.

Tunc salutant peccarium,
et laudaht tabernarium,
excluditur denarius,
profertur sermo varius:

Deu sal misir bescher de vin.
Tunc eum osculamur.
Wir enahten niht uf den Rin,
sed Bacho famulamur.

Tunc rorant scyphi desuper,
et canna pluit mustum,
et qui potaverit nuper,
bibat plus quam sit iustum.

Tunc postulantur tessere,
pro poculis iactatur,
nec de furore Boree
quicquam premeditatur.

But when defeat
Is most complete
Bacchus is still consoling.

Then they hail the wine-bowl's glory,
Toast our host with oratory,
While instead of shillings proffered
Various gems of speech are offered:

"Fill up, the wine is on the house,"
We kiss him then and swallow.
"We bar the Rhine from our carouse,"
But Bacchus, him we follow.

Then cups aloft bedew the floor,
The spigot pours a shower of must,
And he who has drunk eagerly before
Now drinks more than is just.

Then everybody calls for dice
And throws a round or two for drinks;
What wintry winds may blow, what breaths of ice,
Scarce anybody thinks.

Cum In Orbem Universum

Cum in orbem universum
decantatur: "Ite,"
sacerdotes ambulant,
currunt cenobite,
et ab evangelio
iam surgunt levite,
sectam nostram subeunt,
que salus est vite.

In secta nostra scriptum est:
"Omnia probate,
vitam nostram optime
vos considerate;
contra pravos clericos
vos perseverate,
qui non large tribuunt
vobis in caritate."

Marchiones, Bawari,
Saxones, Australes,
quotquot estis, nobiles
vos precor sodales,
auribus percipite
novas decretales:
quod avari pereant
et non liberales.

Et nos misericordie
nunc sumus auctores,
quia nos recipimus
magnos et minores,
recipimus et divites
et pauperiores,
quos devoti monachi
dimittunt extra fores.

Nos recipimus monachum
cum rasa corona,
et si venerit presbiter
cum sua matrona,

Song Of The Vagrant Order

When through all the realms of earth
"Go ye out" resounded,
Priests began to gad about,
Monks with rapture bounded,
Deacons from the Evangels rose,
Weary of redundance —
One and all our order join,
Seeking life's abundance.

In our order it is writ:
"Take all things and try them,
Seek for the best things of life,
See you profit by them.
Wicked priests must rouse your zeal,
Be their stern despisers
If when you demand a dole
They behave like misers."

Austrians, Bavarians,
Saxons, ay, and Mark-men,
Good companions as ye are,
I entreat ye, hark, men!
Hear these new decretals, then
Be their staunch defenders:
Death to penny-pinching men
And not liberal spenders.

We ourselves are fountains where
Bounty never stagnates,
Since we welcome to our ranks
Lesser men and magnates;
We relieve the rich of care,
Give the poor a fresh hold,
Lazars such as godly monks
Banish from their threshold.

We receive the shaven skull
Gladly as the hairy,
When a priest elopes or monk
Bolts the monastery;

magistrum cum pueris,
clerum cum persona,
scolarem libentius
tectum veste bona.

Secta nostra recipit
iustos et iniustos,
claudos atque debiles,
fortes et robustos,
florentes etatibus,
senio onustos,
frigidos et Veneris
ignibus combustos.

Bellosos, pacificos,
mites et insanos,
Boemos, Teutonicos,
Sclavos et Romanos,
stature mediocres,
gigantes et nanos,
in personis humiles
et e contra vanos.

Ordo procul dubio
noster secta vocatur,
quam diversi generis
populus sectatur;
ergo hic et hec et hoc
ei preponatur,
quod sit omnis generis,
qui tot hospitatur.

De vagorum ordine
dico vobis iura,
quorum vita nobilis,
dulcis est natura,
quorum delectat animos
pinguis assatura,
revera plus quam faciat
hordei mensura.

Ordo noster prohibet
matutinas plane:
sunt quedam fantasmata,
que vagantur mane,

Boys from school and masters too,
Parsons, clerks — we're flattered!
But your scholar is our prize,
Clad in robes untattered.

Righteous or unrighteous, we
In our corps enlist them,
Lame and feeble, brave and strong,
All alike subsist them;
Some are in the flower of youth,
Some with age are stricken,
Some are cold of heart, and some,
Warmed by Venus, quicken.

Warmongers and pacifists,
Mild men and demonic,
Roman and Bohemian,
Slavic and Teutonic:
Men of medium size we take,
Likewise dwarfs and giants,
Humble folk, and those who still
Bid the gods defiance.

Truly then our order ranks
As a sect or nation,
Since so many kinds of men
Find here a vocation.
Hic, haec, hoc, he, she, and it,
Here can take their places,
Hospitality like ours
Joins all creeds and races.

Of the vagrant order's laws
These are fundamental:
Generous must we be in life,
In demeanor gentle;
Also we must love a roast,
Dripping unctuous juices,
More than pecks of barley-meal
Fit for a hermit's uses.

Matins next our rule forbids,
Fie on early waking!
Eerie phantoms always prowl
Just as day is breaking,

per que nobis veniunt
visiones vane;
sic qui tunc surrexerit,
non est mentis sane.

Ordo noster prohibet
semper matutinas,
sed statim, cum surgimus,
querimus pruinas;
illuc ferri facimus
vinum et galinas,
nil hic expavescimus
preter hashardi minas.

Ordo noster prohibet
uti dupla veste,
tunicam qui recipit,
ut vadat vix honeste,
pallium mox reicit
Decio conteste,
cingulum huic detrahit
ludus manifeste.

Quod de summis dicitur,
ad imis teneatur,
camisia qui fruitur,
braccis non utatur;
caliga si sequitur,
calceus non feratur;
nam qui hoc transgreditur,
excommunicatur.

Nemo prorsus exeat
hospitium ieiunus,
et si pauper fuerit,
semper petat munus,
incrementum recipit
sepe nummus unus,
cum ad ludum sederit
lusor opportunus.

Nemo in itinere
contrarius sit ventis,
nec quis a paupertate
ferat vultum dolentis,

Causing visions that entail
Direful consequences;
He who rises with the dawn
Hardly has his senses.

So our order interdicts
Matins now and ever;
When we rise, the chimney nook
Claims our first endeavor,
There let serve a bird with wine,
Mixing pleasant prattle,
We have nought to fear from fate
Till the dice-cups rattle.

Last, our order interdicts
All superfluous clothing;
One who sports an overcoat
We must view with loathing.
Let him pledge his needless wrap
At the shrine of Decius,
Soon his vest will follow too —
Dice are avaricious.

What I've said of outer clothes
Holds as well of inner:
Stake your drawers if you've a shirt —
Courage makes a winner;
Why, if boots go up the spout,
For your socks be heedful?
You will certainly be damned
If you lack the needful.

None of us must leave an inn
Till his hunger's sated,
Let him beg a penny too
If necessitated;
There's a chance the small, despised
Coin your needs importune.
May, if played by skillful hands,
Swell into a fortune.

None must ever take the road
When the wind's contrary,
Nor present a doleful face
If his prospects vary.

sed spem sibi proponat
semper consulentis,
nam post malum sequitur
grande sors gaudentis.

Ad quos preveneritis,
his dicatis, quare
singulorum cupitis
mores exprobare:
"Reprobare reprobos
et probos probare,
et probos ab improbis
veni segregare."

Let him keep a cheerful heart,
Hopes are sure to brighten,
When the sky is darkest, then
It can only lighten.

Give to any folk you meet
Reasons for your questing,
As that men's peculiar ways
Seem in need of testing:
"Probity from pravity
Seeking to unravel,
Reprobates to reprobate,
That is why I travel."

Hircus Quando Bibit

Hircus quando bibit,
que non sunt debita dicit,
cum bene potatur,
que non sunt debita fatur.
Cum bene sum potus,
tunc versibus effluo totus.
Cum sicco siccor,
nec in hic, nec in hec, nec in hoc cor.

No Pot, No Poet

When he drinks the lewd clodhopper
Uses language most improper;
When he's altogether pickled,
Then by uncouth deeds he's tickled.
When I'm in my cups my curse is
That I simply slobber verses;
But I'm quickly sick of *hic* or
Haec or *hoc* when lacking liquor.

THE LAST OF GOLIAS

If it is safe to base conclusions on surviving manuscripts, the myth of Golias as titular head of the vagabond order and jocular incarnation of the libertine spirit attained its greatest popularity in England and lasted the longest there. Early in the thirteenth century Giraldus Cambrensis referred to Golias as an actual person, calling him a "lickspittle notorious for gluttony and lecherousness" (*parasitus, gulositate et leccacitate famossissimus*). But the twenty poems ascribed to Golias by their rubrics do not disclose a consistent personality, either real or imaginary. Among them may be found the *Dives eram* by Primas and the *Estuans intrinsecus* by the Archpoet, the latter now naturalized by being addressed to the Bishop of Coventry. The majority of Golias poems in England, however, were not written in the character of outcast clerk or mendicant scholar, but were outspoken satires directed against the corruptions of the clergy. In these Golias, who had once figured as a lineal ancestor of Pantagruel, appears somewhat incongruously as a champion of virtue. In the *Apocalypse of Golias*, which retained its vogue until Elizabeth's reign and was several times translated into English, he lent his name to a savage attack on ecclesiastics of all descriptions, from the Pope down. The monks were the special target of a second piece called the *Metamorphosis of Golias*, the writer's ire having been stirred by their attempts under the leadership of Bernard of Clairvaux to suppress freedom of philosophical speculation. It is not certain that either of these poems was originally written in England, but a reforming zeal which may be considered typically English breathes in several of the lesser satirical pieces.

The two poems here translated are lighter examples of the Golias tradition in England. In one a scamp who describes himself as "goliardus non bastardus" recommends a boon companion to the favor of all the tosspots on the Continent. In the other Golias posing as a mock bishop excommunicates an unknown thief who has purloined his cap. These trifles bid fair to outlast the virulence and indecency of Goliardic satire.

Omnibus In Gallia

Omnibus in Gallia Anglus Goliardus,
obediens et humilis frater non bastardus,
Goliae discipulis, dolens quod tam tardus,
mandat salutem fratribus nomine Ricardus.

Scribo vobis timide tanquam vir ignotus,
qui tamen dum vixero vester ero totus;
deprecor attentius, supplex et devotus,
Goliardus fieri, non vilis harlotus.

Accedit ad vos nuncius vir magnae probitatis,
magister et dominus Willelmus de Conflatis,
Goliardus optimus, hoc non timeatis;
sicut decet socium ipsum admittatis,
quicquid de me dixerit verum teneatis,
et quod volueritis per eum rescribatis;
quae mihi scripseritis vel ore mandatis,
pro posse meo faciam certissime sciatis.

De adventu nobilis nuncii gaudete;
villam quam intraverit in illa manete,
et hora cum fuerit cum ipso prandete,
mero delectabili calices implete;
tempus cum sit frigidum ad prunas sedete;
vinum meracissimum manibus tenete;
calices si fuerint vacui, replete;
ut bibat et rebibat saepe suadete.
Si bene potaverit, certum tunc habete,
vobiscum moram faciet libenter et laete,
in bursa dum repererit staterem monetae,
et donec haustae fuerint quindecim metretae.
Modum si excesserit, blande sustinete;
quod fit in consortio pandere cavete.

Nunc, fratres karissimi, scribere studete,
ordo vester qualis est modusque dietae;
si fas est comedere coctas in lebete
carnas, vel pisciculos fugatos ad rete;

To The Brethren In France

Richard, an English brother, a Goliard and no bastard,
A man submissive to command whom pride has never mastered,
With sorrow for his long delay your pardon now entreating,
To all the brotherhood in France who follow Golias: Greeting!

Although I write with diffidence, as best befits a stranger,
Yet trust me, I am yours for life in trials or in danger;
And first I beg with downcast eyes, hands joined, and heart
     a-flutter,
Believe me a true Goliard, not a rakehell from the gutter.

A man of utmost probity shall be my message-bearer:
William of Conflans, lord and sire, goes forth, a stout wayfarer;
A genuine Goliard is he, no other name will fit him,
Fear not to welcome him and to your fellowship admit him.
Whatever he shall say from me, think not I will gainsay it,
And what you write me, give to him and he will reconvey it;
And anything you bid me do, by word of mouth or writing,
Be sure I shall perform it, not the least commission slighting.

When this most noble messenger shall come, be glad to greet him,
Whatever town he enters, let a royal welcome meet him,
And at the hour of dinner bid him share your ordinary;
Ply him with cups of choicest wine — I charge you be not chary.
In frosty weather let him sit snug in your chimney-corner,
And hand him no diluted draught, for nothing is forlorner.
Whenever cups are empty, quick! the vacancy replenish,
And bid him drink and drink again good Burgundy and Rhenish.
When he has lined his belly well, then you may take for granted
The more you press him to remain the more he'll be enchanted;
He'll never move to leave you while his pocket holds a stiver,
And had you fifteen casks to drain, he'd be the last survivor.
If he exceeds all measure, underprop him when he staggers;
But what happens at the party, keep it safely from tongue-
     waggers.

For an answer, dearest brothers, I'll most eagerly be looking:
Please tell me all your order's news, especially what's cooking.
Do they allow you any meat to meliorate the kettle,
Or is it only little fish that in your flesh-pots settle?

de Lyaeo bibere vel de unda Thetae;
utrum frui liceat Rosa vel Agnete;
cum formosa domina ludere secrete;
continenter vivere nullatenus iubete.

Qualiter me debeam gerere docete,
ne magis in ordine vivam indiscrete;
donec ad vos veniam, sum sine quiete: —
quid vobis dicam amplius? — In Domino valete!

Summa salus omnium, filius Mariae,
pascat, potet, vestiat pueros Golyae!
et conservet socios sanctae confratriae,
ad dies usque ultimos Enoch et Helyae! — Amen.

And do you quaff Lyaean juice or lap the wave of Thetis?
And do you sleep with Agnes, Rose, or any other sweeties?
For your game with lovely woman, sure, is more than senti-
  mental;
To lead a life of continence, who cares a continental?

Now teach me what I ought to do to live in most disorder
That I may win an honorable title in your order;
Until I come to visit you, I take no thought of sleeping. —
What more is there for me to say? — Lord have you in his
  keeping.

So may our Savior, Mary's son, to Golias' retainers
Give food and drink and proper clothes, that they may rest the
  gainers.
And grant that all good fellows in this brotherhood so pious
May flourish in the latter day with Enoch and Elias. — AMEN.

Raptor Mei Pilei

Raptor mei pilei morte moriatur,
mors sit subitanea, nec praevideatur,
et poena continua post mortem sequatur,
nec campis Elysiis post Lethen fruatur.

Raptor mei pilei saeva morte cadat,
illum febris, rabies, et tabes invadat;
hunc de libro Dominus vitae sanctae radat;
hunc tormentis Aeacus cruciandum tradat.

Ei vita brevis sit, pessimusque finis!
nec vivat foeliciter hic diebus binis;
laceret hunc Cerberus dentibus caninis,
laceratum gravius torqueat Erinnys.

Nunquam diu baiulet illi colum Cloto;
cesset filo Lachesis tracto nondum toto;
filum rumpat Atropos, nec fruatur voto,
et miser presbytero corruat remoto.

Excommunicatus sit in agro et tecto!
nullus eum videat lumine directo!
solus semper sedeat similis deiecto:
hunc poenis Tartareis cruciet Alecto.

Ille rebus omnibus quas habet emunctus,
nec confessus occidat, oleo nec unctus,
morte subitanea palleat defunctus,
Iudae traditori sit inferno coniunctus.

Hoc si quis audierit excommunicamen,
et non observaverit praesulis examen;
nisi resipuerit corrigens peccamen,
anathema fuerit! fiat, fiat. AMEN.

Golias Curses A Thief

The thief who stole my cap — may he die a mean death!
May he die more abundantly, as the Bible saith,
Be suddenly cut down like grass that withereth,
And take a painful leave soon of his last breath.

The thief who stole my cap — blast him to futurity!
May he not live two days to gloat in his security.
May death afford him agonies of excruciating purity,
And may he suffer after death with inexorable surety.

May fever, madness, wasting, and all plagues blight him.
May God from the Book of Life exclude him to requite him.
May not a single breath from Paradise delight him,
But when he gets to Hell, may the hell-hounds bite him.

May fate no more uphold him, but drop him in the mire.
Of spinning out his life may the dark sisters tire.
May his thread be broken short, ere he gain his desire,
And let him to a hedge-priest fall, and wretchedly expire.

May he lack in house and field the Church's protection:
Let no one dare to look at him except by indirection.
May he sit and sulk in solitude, a symbol of dejection,
And may the Devil toast him as Hell's choicest confection.

May his goods be stolen from him without any compunction.
May he die unconfessed, without blessing or unction.
May he meet the pale rider, and fail in every function,
And be gathered to Judas in appropriate conjunction.

If any man shall hear this excommunication
And fail to bow before the bishop's proclamation,
Unless he repent, he must bear our execration:
Anathema maranatha! which means his sure damnation.
                              Fiat! fiat! AMEN.

EPILOGUE

Songs of spring in good measure were included in the Benedictbeuern Manuscript, but the love song which follows, distinguished by its autumnal imagery, was somehow overlooked. It has been preserved fortunately in a thirteenth century manuscript now in the Bibliothèque Nationale at Paris, to remind us that, as Keats tells us, autumn has its music too. Anyone who has experienced the somber setting in of winter in France, the browning of the earth, the sun vanished from a darkened sky, the incessant rains, the inescapable and all pervading chill, must agree that the writer of this lyric was an excellent observer. Not less remarkable than the opening lines, however, is the statement of the lover's passion, where a world-old theme is freshened by sincerity of sensation and a quaint grace of style. Not often in poetry can one find, as here, a perfect equivalent to the effect on the palate of a light dry claret.

In looking back over the Goliardic poems, perhaps their most astonishing quality is their success in sustaining clear unmixed emotional tones. Nothing that we know of the writers of these lyrics would justify us in supposing that they led more sheltered lives than poets of any other age. Their world no less than ours was afflicted by sickness, hunger, sudden death, heartbreak, and injustice. They were abundantly aware of these things, and in the mood of satire raged and lamented because of them. But they possessed a childlike power to free the mind from the dregs of bitterness, and in their moments of gaiety there was no tinge of regret or foreboding. To attain such purity of tone was an achievement. The savor of life is lost when, as in much romantic poetry, all the emotions are stewed in the same pot, nor is the world any the better when the sharp contrasts of ecstasy and wretchedness are dulled to a prevailing drabness. In defending the present hour from the intrusions of before and after the Goliards showed a sure esthetic instinct.

De Ramis Cadunt Folia

De ramis cadunt folia,
nam viror totus periit;
iam calor liquit omnia
    et abiit;
nam signa celi ultima
    sol petiit.

Iam nocet frigus teneris,
et avis bruma leditur,
et philomena ceteris
    conqueritur,
quod illis ignis etheris
    adimitur.

Nec lympha caret alveus,
nec prata virent herbida;
sol nostra fugit aureus
    confinia;
est inde dies niveus,
    nox frigida.

Modo frigescit, quicquid est,
sed solus ego caleo;
immo sic mihi cordi est
    quod ardeo;
hic ignis tamen virgo est,
    qual angueo.

Nutritur ignis osculo
et leni tactu virginis;
in suo lucet oculo
    lux luminis,
nec est in toto seculo
    plus numinis.

Ignis grecus extinguitur
cum vino iam acerrimo;
sed iste non extinguitur
    miserrimo;
immo fomento alitur
    uberrimo.

Autumnal

The dead leaves from the boughs are cast
And greenness fades from trees and vines,
For once the summer heats have passed
    All nature pines;
And now the sun draws near the last
    Of heavenly signs.

The cold is death to tender things.
Winter's the season birds condemn;
Now Philomel for her kindred sings
    A requiem;
The solar fire that warmed their wings
    Burns low for them.

Now every hollow oozes wet
When fields of withered grass are crossed;
The golden sun remains as yet
    A truant lost,
Hence days of snow we're like to get
    And nights of frost.

Now that whatever is must freeze,
Pity that I alone should burn
And that consuming fires should seize
    My heart in turn:
A girl's the cause of flames like these,
    For her I yearn.

The light touch of a maiden's hand,
Her kisses too, they feed the fire,
Her eyes, the light of lights, are bland
    To wake desire,
Nor have I known on sea or land
    A power higher.

Greek fire may be put out if drenched
In wine as sour as it can be,
The flame I feel can ne'er be quenched,
    Worse luck for me!
Its fuel from my heart is wrenched
    Incessantly.

A BOOK LIST AND SOME NOTES

History and Criticism. The standard work is by the German scholar Max Manitius, *Geschichte des lateinischen Literatur des Mittelalters* (1911–31). A close equivalent in English is F. J. E. Raby's *History of Christian Latin Poetry* (1927) and *History of Secular Latin Poetry of the Middle Ages* (1934), both of which are authoritative and readable. Helen Waddell's *The Wandering Scholars* (1927) is an excellent popular book by a scholar with a fine sense of style. P. S. Allen's *The Romanesque Lyric* (1928) and *Medieval Latin Lyrics* (1931) are effervescent with confused erudition and contain distinguished translations by Howard Mumford Jones. John Addington Symonds' essay (see under Anthologies) still affords amusing reading, but a more accurate and informative short chapter is included in J. A. MacCulloch's *Medieval Faith and Fable* (1932). Special studies by J. M. Manly, "Familia Goliae," *Modern Philology*, V (1907–08), 201ff., and J. H. Hanford, "The Progenitors of Golias," *Speculum*, I (1926), 38–58, are not too technical for general reading. The cultural background is well given by C. H. Haskins in *The Renaissance of the Twelfth Century* (1933).

Anthologies. The pioneer translator of Goliardic verse was John Addington Symonds, whose *Wine, Women and Song* (1884) has become a minor classic. It does not contain the original Latin. *The Oxford Book of Medieval Latin Verse* (1928) by Stephen Gaselee, contains 111 poems, both religious and secular, ranging from the fourth to the fifteenth century. Less than twenty of these are in the Goliardic vein. Helen Waddell's *Medieval Latin Lyrics* (1929) covers some twelve centuries, beginning with the Virgilian Copa, and includes 29 poems from the Benedictbeuern Manuscript as well as other secular verse. An expert selection from the work of the wandering scholars has been made by Max Manitius in *Vagantenlieder* (Jena, 1927) with German verse translations by Robert Ulich. A similar but inferior book is *Les Poésies des Goliards* (Paris, 1929) by Olga Dobiache-Rojdesvensky, which has French prose translations facing the Latin, and which includes much more poetry in satirical vein than can be found elsewhere.

Notes. Sources of the text, previous translations, and various other matters. Books repeatedly referred to will be designated briefly as follows:

CB — *Carmina Burana*, edited by Schmeller, J. A., 1847.

S — Symonds, J. A., *Wine, Women and Song*, 1884.

V — Ulich, R., and Manitius, M., *Vagantenlieder aus der lateinischen Dichtung des 12. und 13. Jahrhunderts*, 1927.

W1 — Waddell, Helen, *The Wandering Scholars*, 1927.

A1 — Allen, P. S., *The Romanesque Lyric*, 1928. With translations by Howard Mumford Jones.

W2 — Waddell, Helen, *Medieval Latin Lyrics*, 1929.

CB2 — *Carmina Burana*, edited by Hilka, A., and Schumann, W., 1930 (incomplete).

A2 — Allen, P. S., *Medieval Latin Lyrics*, 1931. With translations by Jones.

SEDULIUS SCOTTUS. Text from Traube, L., *Poetae Latini Aevi Carolini*, Vol. III. Critical analysis by Jarcho, B. I., "Die Vorläufer des Golias," *Speculum*, III (1928), pp. 523ff.

Flamina nos Boreae. Translation, omitting last six lines, in A2, p. 102.

Nunc viridant segetes. Translation in W2, p. 121.

Tado, benigne vidi. Translation of last ten lines only in W2, p. 119.

Nos sitis atque fames. Not previously translated. Traube glosses *tenuida* (l. 9) as *Dünnbier*.

Aut lego vel scribo. Translation in W2, p. 123.

THE CAMBRIDGE SONGS. Text from Breul, K., *The Cambridge Songs*, 1915. See also Strecker, K., *Die Cambridger Lieder*, 1926, for different readings. In this section, and in all that follow with the exception of that headed The Last of Golias, the texts consistently use a plain letter *e* where *ae* or *oe* would be used in classical Latin.

Vestiunt silve. The accentual Sapphics of the original I have rendered in what by courtesy are called "English Sapphics," the meter of Channing's "Needy Knife-Grinder." A translation from Strecker's text in W2, p. 143.

In vitis patrum veterum. This poem is by Fulbert of Chartres. Translations in A1, p. 285; W1, p. 89.

Iam, dulcis amica. The word *sola* in the third from the last stanza indicates that the speaker at this point is the girl. Translations in S, p. 14; A1, p. 288; and from Strecker's text in W2, p. 145.

Levis exsurgit Zephyrus. Referred to by Robert Frost in "The Lesson for Today," *A Witness Tree*, p. 46. Translations in A1, p. 290; W2, p. 157.

AUTHOR UNKNOWN, POSSIBLY PETER ABELARD. For a discussion of these learned lyrics as a group, see Professor Allen's *Medieval Latin Lyrics*, pp. 243ff.

Dum Diane vitrea. CB No. 37. Text of stanzas 1–4 as given in V; stanza 6 as emended by Allen (A2, p. 247). Translations in S, p. 107; W2, p. 265, omitting stanzas 5 and 7.

Olim sudor Herculis. CB No. 38. Not previously translated. Iole: the boy Iolas, Hercules' page, has by a not unnatural mis-understanding been transformed into a mistress. The various exploits of Hercules referred to in the poem may be found in a classical dictionary.

Axe Phebus aureo. CB No. 44. Not previously translated. Cybele: the earth goddess. Semele's favored son: Bacchus. The passage has been conjecturally restored.

Clausus Chronos. CB No. 46. Translation in W2, p. 243. Miss Waddell emends the last two lines to read:

> et quibus es Venus,
> es et Dione.

I have so translated. I suspect that the previous verse also should be regarded as addressed to Venus and the verbs changed to the second person singular. Note *pandit* where the rhyme demands *pandis*.

Si linguis angelicis. CB No. 50. Not previously translated. For a discussion of the relation of this remarkable poem to the *Roman de la Rose*, see Langlois, E., *Les Origines et Sources du Roman de la Rose*, 1891.

Sevit aure spiritus. CB No. 56. Translation in S, p. 130. The word *sole* in line 4 makes sense, but *solo* makes both sense and rhyme, and I have accordingly adopted it.

Rumor letalis. CB No. 83 (where the first word is given wrongly as *Humor*). Text from Gaselee, S., *The Oxford Book of Medieval Verse*. Translation in S, p. 144; also Kenneth Rexroth, *The Phoenix and the Tortoise*, p. 89.

Hebet sidus. CB No. 131. Text from V. Translation in A2, p. 107.

HUGO OF ORLEANS (PRIMAS). Text from W. Meyer (aus Speyer), "Die Oxforder Gedichte des Primas," *Nach. v. d. Kgl. Gesellsch. d. Wissen. zu Göttingen*, Phil.–hist. Kl., 1907. Nos. 1, 2, 15, and 23. None of these poems has previously been translated.

Hospes erat. "Primas perdidit v. solidos": pronounce *vau*, not *quinque.*

Vir pietatis inops. Briareus was the hundred-handed giant of classical mythology. There were two tyrants of Syracuse named Dionysius, and both were said to be huge in stature. Primas is small like Zaccheus, who "climbed a tree his Lord to see."

Dives eram et dilectus. Primas is supposed to be speaking to the canons of Orleans. He has taken the part of a crippled inmate of the guest house against a bully of a chaplain and his satellite William, and has been himself ejected in consequence. As in the preceding poem, the action is told several times over with increments each time.

THE ARCHPOET OF COLOGNE. Text from M. Manitius, *Die Gedichte des Archipoeta*, 1913, with exceptions noted in the second poem below. The original Latin of the stanzas quoted in the headnote is from poem No. VI and reads as follows:

> Poeta pauperior omnibus poetis,
> nichil prorsus habeo, nisi quod videtis.
> Unde sepe lugeo, quando vos ridetis;
> nec me meo vitio pauperem putetis.

Fodere non debeo, quia sum scolaris,
ortus ex militibus preliandi gnaris;
sed quia me terruit labor militaris,
malui Virgilium sequi quam te, Paris.

Mendicare pudor est, mendicare nolo,
fures multa possident, sed non absque dolo.
Quid ergo iam faciam, qui nec agros colo,
nec mendicus fieri nec fur esse volo.

Sepe de miseria mee paupertatis
conqueror in carmine viris litteratis;
laici non capiunt ea, que sunt vatis,
et nil me retribuunt, quod est notum satis.

Omnia tempus habent. This poem invites comparison with the
Pontificum spuma of Primas, both being exercises in leonine or rhymed
hexameters. I doubt if this verse form can even be approximated in
English, but that has not kept me from trying. Not previously
translated.

Estuans intrinsecus. Often called *Confessio Goliae.* The famous
stanza beginning, "Meum est propositum in taberna mori," I
have given in its most familiar form from T. Wright, *The Latin Poems
Commonly Attributed to Walter Mapes*, p. 73. The version approved by
Manitius runs:

> Meum est propositum in taberna mori,
> ut sint vina proxima morientis ori;
> tunc cantabunt letius angelorum chori:
> "Sit deus propitius huic potatori."

Stanzas 26–30 occur only in CB No. CLXXII, and are regarded as
spurious. I have accordingly placed them in brackets. Translations
in S, p. 65; W2, p. 171.

Fama tuba dante sonum. The sonority of the opening lines suggests
the tremendous roll of the *Dies Irae,* but the latter poem did not
attain its final form till nearly a century after the Archpoet. Vienna
in line 6 is not the capital of Austria, but Vienne in southeastern
France. Not previously translated.

WALTER OF CHATILLON. Text of the first three poems from K.
Strecker, *Die Lieder Walters von Chatillon,* 1925; of the last two from
the same editor's *Moralisch-Satirische Gedichte Walters von Chatillon,*
1929. None of these poems has previously been translated.

Importuna Veneri. Readings in last stanza from S. Gaselee, *The
Oxford Book of Medieval Latin Verse,* p. 131.

Versa est in luctum. CB No. LXXXVI. I have taken "vilitatem
morbi" as a reference to the leprosy of which the poet died.

Dum Galterus egrotaret. One stanza from a poem of 150 lines.

CARMINA BURANA: SATIRE AND MORALITY.

Florebat olim studium. Text from CB2. Not previously translated. Mary and Martha are familiar as types of the contemplative and the active life. Leah was supposed to be especially prolific. Rachel's eyes, bright with tears, were famous for their beauty. Cato was of course a synonym for rigid virtue and Lucrece for chastity.

Manus ferens munera. Text from CB2, where this poem is assigned the first place in the collection. It was long popular. I have preferred the order of stanzas given by Wright. The play on ablative, dative, genitive at the end of stanza 4 has implications which I have intentionally obliterated in English. Not previously translated.

Ecce sonat in aperto. CB No. LXXIII. Text from V. CB2 gives a few additional stanzas which I have not used. Not previously translated.

Iste mundus. CB No. VI. Translation in S, p. 184.

Dum iuventus floruit. CB No. X. Translation in S, p. 182.

Quod spiritu David. CB No. XXIV. Text from V, which omits the third of the four stanzas. CB2 rearranges and amplifies the poem. Not previously translated.

Veritas veritatum. CB No. III (a fragment). CB2 gives the entire poem. Translation in W2, p. 197.

CARMINA BURANA: SPRINGTIME AND LOVE.

Ianus annum circinat. CB No. 31. Not previously translated.

Amor habet superos. CB No. 61 (text very corrupt). I have used the text given by W. Meyer, "Zwei mittellateinische Lieder in Florenz," *Studi letterari e linguistici dedicati a Pio Rajna,* 1911, but have moved the fourth stanza to sixth place quite arbitrarily for the sake of better coherence. Translation (if it can be called that) in S, p. 137.

Anni novi rediit novitas. CB No. 51. Translations in S, p. 89; W2, p. 257.

Letabundus rediit. CB No. 47. Text from V. Translation in W2, p. 215.

Omittamus studia. CB No. 48. Apparently two lines from stanza 1 are missing. Translations in S, p. 99; W2, p. 203.

Vacillantis trutine. CB No. 159 (a fragment). Complete poem in W. Meyer, "Die Arundel Sammlung mittellateinischer Lieder," *Abh. d. Kgl. Gesellsch. d. Wissen. zu Göttingen,* XI (1909), p. 29. Not previously translated.

Lingua mendax et dolosa. CB No. 168. Translation in S, p. 141.

Sic mea fata canendo. CB No. 167. Translations in S, p. 139; W2, p. 269.

O comes amoris. CB No. 162 (two stanzas only). Complete text given by W. Meyer, *Fragmenta Burana,* 1901. Miss Waddell, taking the poem romantically, defends the readings found in the two-stanza version. The longer version falls over into comedy somewhat akin to the seventeenth-century song of *Phillida Flouts Me.* Translations (two stanzas only) in S, p. 149; W2, p. 255.

Tempus instat floridum. Text by Allen in *Modern Philology*, VI (1909), p. 91. German scholarship holds that the *Natureingang* is an excrescence added to the poem, but artistically it could not well be spared. Translation (without the opening lines) in S, p. 147.

Exiit diluculo. CB No. 63. Translation in S, p. 102. The last line should probably read: "I mecum ludere." Symonds preserves the Victorian proprieties by putting this speech into the mouth of the scholar.

Musa venit carmine. CB No. 108. Translations in S, p. 94 (last verse only); W2, p. 239.

Cedit, hyems. CB No. 98 Translations in S, p. 80; W2, p. 211.

Omnia sol temperat. CB No. 99. Translation in S, p. 90.

Ver redit optatum. CB. No. 100. Translation in S, p. 75.

Iamiam rident prata. CB No. 107. Translations in S, p. 81; W2, p. 213. I have rearranged as three lines the second and third lines of stanza 1, which originally stood thus:

> iamiam virgines iocundantur,
> terre ridet facies.

Salve ver optatum. CB No. 118. Translations in S, p. 85; W2, p. 233.

Veris dulcis in tempore. CB No. 121. Translation in S, p. 92.

Dum estas inchoatur. CB No. 122. Translations in S, p. 88; W2, p. 263.

Vere dulci mediante. CB No. 120. Text from V. Not previously translated.

Laboris remedium. CB No. 129. Text from V. Not previously translated. The opening lines echo a hymn to the Virgin.

Tempus est iucundum. CB No. 140. Text from V. Translations in S, p. 76; W2, p. 223.

Stetit puella. Two stanzas from CB No. 138. Translation in W1, p. 207.

CARMINA BURANA: TAVERN AND OPEN ROAD

Tempus hoc letitie. CB No. 190. Text from V. Not previously translated.

Exul ego clericus. CB No. XCI. Text from V. Translation in S, p. 59.

In taberna quando sumus. CB No. 175. Text from V. The second stanza only is translated in S, p. 155. Certain lines parody a hymn by Thomas Aquinas.

Bacche, benevenies. CB No. 178. Not previously translated.

Potatores exquisiti. CB No. 179. Translations in S, p. 173; W2, p. 185 (unsurpassable).

Denudata veritate. CB No. 173 (incomplete). Text of first eleven and one half stanzas from V; the remainder from E. DuMéril, *Poésies inédites du moyen âge*, 1854, p. 303. Translation in S., p. 165.

Didymus is another name for "doubting Thomas." The stanza that should follow immediately after Didymus is half missing in the original, and I have omitted it entirely. On the subject of these debates in general, see Hanford, J. H., "The Medieval Debate between Wine and Water," *Pub. Mod. Lang. Assn. of Am.*, XXVII (1913), pp. 315ff.

Alte clamat Epicurus. CB No. CLXXXVI. Text from V. Not previously translated.

Olim latus colueram. CB No. 92. Translation in S, p. 176.

Dum caupona verterem. CB No. 49. Text from V. Not previously translated. Metrically this poem seems to be related to *Si linguis angelicis*, though very different in spirit.

O Fortuna. CB No. 1. Not previously translated.

Si quis Deciorum. CB No. 174. Not previously translated. The piece seems to be a late and spiritless combination of snatches from other poems, but I include it because it contains all the standard jests on gambling. My rendering of the two lines in French-German jargon is purely psychic, since I can make out only about half the words.

Cum in orbem. CB No. 193. Text from R. Peiper, *Gaudeamus*, with some readings from V. I have added stanza 10 from CB as stanza 8 of the present arrangement.

Hircus quando bibit. CB No. 182a. Not previously translated. So far as I know the poetry of hiccoughing begins and ends with this piece.

THE LAST OF GOLIAS. Text from T. Wright, *The Latin Poems Commonly Attributed to Walter Mapes*, 1841. Neither poem has previously been translated. In this section *ae* and *oe* are given in full, not simply represented as *e*.

Raptor mei pilei. I have substituted Christian figures for classical whenever possible: Alecto becomes the Devil, Cerberus hell-hounds, and so on.

EPILOGUE

De ramis cadunt folia. This poem might have been included in *Carmina Burana*, but wasn't. Text from E. DuMéril, *Poésies populaires latines du moyen âge, 1847*. Translations in A2, p. 73; W2, p. 275.

INDEX OF LATIN POEMS

(*First Lines*)

[301]

INDEX OF ENGLISH POEMS

(*Titles*)

New Directions Paperbooks

Complete descriptive catalog available free on request from
New Directions, 333 Sixth Avenue, New York 10014.   † Bilingual.